Handbook for Multi-Sensory Worship

•

Handbook for Multi-Sensory Worship

Kim Miller
and the Ginghamsburg Church Worship Team

Abingdon Press
Nashville

HANDBOOK FOR MULTI-SENSORY WORSHIP

Copyright © 1999 by Ginghamsburg Church

All rights reserved.

This book is printed on recycled, acid-free paper.

Library of Congress Cataloging-in-Publication Data

Miller, Kim, 1956-

    Handbook for multi-sensory worship / Kim Miller and the Ginghamsburg Church Worship Team.
       p.   cm.
    Includes appendices.
    ISBN 0-687-06860-6 (alk. paper)
    1. Worship programs.   I. Ginghamsburg United Methodist Church (Dayton, Ohio). Worship Team.
    II. Title.
    BV198.M55   1999
    264—dc21
                                                99-39677
                                                  CIP

Scripture quotations, unless otherwise indicated, are from the New Revised Standard Version Bible, copyright © 1989, by the Division of Christian Education of the National Council of the Churches of Christ in the United States of America.

Scripture taken from *THE MESSAGE.* Copyright © by Eugene H. Peterson, 1993, 1994, 1995. Used by permission of NavPress Publishing Group.

Scripture quotations noted NIV are taken from the *Holy Bible: New International Version.* Copyright © 1973, 1978, 1984 by the International Bible Society. Used by permission of Zondervan Bible Publishers.

99 00 01 02 03 04 05 06 07 08 — 10 9 8 7 6 5 4 3 2 1

MANUFACTURED IN THE UNITED STATES OF AMERICA

Contents

98132

Introduction

Recently while attending a dramatic arts workshop, I took the opportunity to take on the feelings that a prechurched person might have while attending a typical Protestant worship event. Here are the thoughts I wrote down.

"Do me the favor of considering why I'm here.

—It's not to be entertained—you can't compete with my TV.

—It's not to be impressed—you know there's always somebody better out there.

—It's not to be condemned—I feel that already.

The only reason I'm here is my deep unspoken hope of connecting with God and my God-destiny."

Worship celebrations designed to speak to today's culture must be planned for the purpose of connecting people to God and their God-destiny. That's why we've developed a format for *why* we're putting a celebration together before we plan *how* we will do it. The format includes these elements.

Word: The Word of God, as discerned in the Scripture

Felt Need: The presenting need(s) that the people bring to worship

Desired Outcome: The expected responses that people will make

Theme: The package in which the message is wrapped

Metaphor: The root image that permits the desired outcome to connect with the needs of the people

Structure: The order of worship

When planning our weekly event, we discipline ourselves as a team to thoroughly explore these elements before proceeding with the creative structure itself. This list becomes a constant reminder of how we will connect people to God that week.

The pages of this worship celebration resource are filled with the imaginative efforts of our worship design team at Ginghamsburg Church in Tipp City, Ohio. While all of the components are strong, the hallmark of a great celebration is the combination of the segments, which together with the speaker's message, present truly postmodern forms of storytelling. While these different parts work well together within the themes presented, it is possible to choose from them "cafeteria style" and use individual segments as you wish in your own setting.

Music

The song suggestions are from a wide variety of sources. For popular secular songs (featured or opening music) our band leaders generally find the appropriate CD at a retail store. After purchasing the CD, they can then "lift" the music off the recording by listening and writing words and chords for the band members. Your local CD store is a great resource and their employees can assist in finding the CD using the artist's name as a reference. Many retailers use a computer file and can identify any CD that may have a particular song on it. In addition, you may do an artist search on the Web by going to the individual artist's sites. This may be helpful in locating a particular song and words. Speaking of words, we do change some of the words now and then to suit out own purposes. Of course, the performance on a copywritten song must be limited to the live performance in worship only. We cannot record, sell or reproduce the songs in any way (see copyright laws below).

The musical selections in the Song Celebration segments are those that the entire congregation sing together. While they sometimes follow the theme, more often they were simply favorites of ours at the time. We can't promise that they are available at this time but the possible resources are listed in this handbook. These publishers generally offer written music as well as a recorded version.

Media

A thumbnail image of the main graphic that depicts the metaphor for most of the celebrations can be viewed on the CD that accompanies this book. These graphics are available for purchase via download from the digital store at Cokesbury Online (http://www.cokesbury.com/digitalstore).

In addition to this basic use of media each week, we produce our own "spots" to showcase various ministries or to tell someone's personal story. As these pieces would not be transferable to other congregations, we would encourage churches to produce their own "spots." Some video pieces may be available through our Ginghamsburg bookstore. Please check our web site or call Ginghamsburg Church. To support the theme or message in some way, video clips may also be used off of rented or purchased videos. We have suggested some for you in addition to describing the scene to be used. The basic applicable legal code is buried under Section 110 of the Copyright Law of 1976 (17 U.S.C. & 110 (3)). Section 110 states that, without fear of breaking the law, churches may:

1. Perform nondramatic literary or musical works and religious dramatic and musical works

2. Display individual works of a nonsequential nature (17 U.S.C. & 101).

during services at a house of worship or other religious assembly. "Display," as defined in legalese, means to "show a copy of [a work] either directly or by means of a film, slide, television image, or any other device or process or, in the case of a motion picture or other audiovisual work, to show individual images nonsequentially."

In other words, this means churches may:

1. Perform contemporary songs, regardless of the owner/writer.

2. Show any still image regardless of their sources, and even show frames of a film if they are not in sequence.

For further legal information regarding copyright and reproduction of music, please contact your own lawyer or consider purchasing a copy of Len Wilson's book, *The Wired Church.*

Most of the scripts for the Calls to Worship, Prayers, and Dramas and main graphic images are included; however, a few are not available at this time. Consider this your opportunity to write and add some pieces on your own! We also encourage you to experiment with the visual enhancement and what works best in your particular setting.

This resource for other churches is a wonderful next-step for us. Most of all, however, our hope is that as you gather ideas, you will also catch a glimpse of what a team can design together in the power of God's spirit. We anticipate that your team will discover its own amazing potential to present the timeless story of God's heart toward humankind.

Using the CD-ROM Included with This Book

The CD-ROM included with this book contains a short, interactive demo that will allow you to see examples of the multi-sensory elements incorporated in the worship celebrations at Ginghamsburg. The demo consists of two parts: the interactive teaser and a catalog of images.

Interactive Demo

After a brief introductory video, an image of a desk will appear (this may take a few seconds to load). Explore the items in this "virtual office" by passing your cursor over the various items in the "room." Your cursor will change to the image of a hand when it comes in contact with an interactive object. Click the object to initiate its action. You will want to pay particular attention to these items:

- **Book**: Opens to display examples of graphics
- **Middle desk drawer**: Contains an example of a Call to Worship
- **Clipboard**: Contains an example of a drama
- **Bottom left-hand drawer**: Shows the credits for the production of the interactive teaser
- **Trash can**: Allows you to quit the demo

Catalog of Images

A catalog of worship images that were produced by Ginghamsburg to accompany many of the celebrations in this book is also included on the CD-ROM. These images may be purchased for use in your own church through the Digital Store at Cokesbury Online (*www.cokesbury.com/digitalstore*). Whether or not you choose to purchase any of these graphics, they will hopefully inspire the creative efforts and energies of your own design team!

To view the image catalogs, open the graphics or **Book** icon from the **Main** screen. On the left side of the screen, you will see a series of buttons. Click the **Index** button located at the bottom. This will bring up thumbnail images of the sets of graphics available for purchase. To view all of the images included in a particular set, click on the thumbnail. This will allow you to view a larger version of the image you selected and to see the images included in that particular set. From this screen, you can click through all of the images by using the **Next** and **Back** buttons (located on the left side of the screen), or return to the index page using the **Index** button. To purchase any of these images, follow the instructions listed on the catalog pages.

System Requirements for Viewing the CD-ROM

The interactive demo uses two programs that you may need to install on your machine: QuarkImmedia Viewer and QuickTime 3.0. Both of these programs are included on the CD-ROM. You can run the demo entirely from the CD, but performance may improve if you install the QuarkImmedia Viewer. You must, however, have QuickTime 3.0 or higher installed on your hard drive to run QuarkImmedia, whether from your hard drive or from the CD.

QuarkImmedia Viewer is a stand-alone application that allows anyone to view and interact with QuarkImmedia projects. The QuarkImmedia Viewer is distributed royalty-free. QuarkImmedia Viewer 1.5 is available for Windows, Macintosh, and Power Macintosh. The Windows version is compatible with Windows 95 and 98. You will need a sound card with speakers to fully appreciate the sounds and graphics. Minimum requirements are a pentium processor and 16MB of RAM with 256 colors for the monitor. We have obtained best viewing results with at least a Pentium 166mghz and 32MB of RAM, and at least an 8x CD-ROM.

Installation

QuickTime 4.0:

To install the 32-bit version of QuickTime 4.0 from the CD-ROM:

• Open **My Computer** or **Windows Explorer** (Windows 95 or 98).
• Locate your CD-ROM drive and double-click to view the contents of the CD.
• Double-click the **QuickTimeInstaller.exe** file and follow the installation instructions.

QuarkImmedia Viewer:

Windows: To install QuarkImmedia Viewer on your hard drive, from the **Start** menu (Windows 95 or 98), select **Run, X:\install.exe,** where **X** is the letter of your CD-ROM drive. Close all open applications and follow the on-screen directions. When the viewer is installed, launch it from the program group or desktop. To open the CD-ROM, select **Open** from the **File** menu and select the file called **X:\worship.imd**.

Macintosh: Double-click the **Worship** icon on your desktop to view the contents of the CD-ROM. Open the "QuarkImmedia Viewer for Mac OS" folder and click on the QuarkImmedia Viewer 1.5 icon to install. If you choose not to install the viewer, you can click on the **Worship.imd** file to play the demo directly from the CD.

To Run the Demo from the CD Without Installing QuarkImmedia:

Open **My Computer** or **Windows Explorer** (Windows 95 or 98) and double-click your CD-ROM drive. Double-click the **Worship.imd** file to launch QuarkImmedia Viewer and begin the demo.

To receive technical support for the installation of the CD-ROM, call Abingdon Software technical support at 1-615-749-6777, 8:30 A.M. to 4 P.M. CST, Monday through Friday.

God's Invitation

Felt Need	Love
Desired Outcome	To know God's inclusive heart of love—Belonging
Theme	God's Invitation
Word	2 Samuel 9
Metaphor/Image	Beautiful place setting at a table with a name card
Synopsis	We all have deep needs for love—to know that we are accepted and wanted. The good news is that God has a huge heart of love and wants to include each one of us in the family. The story of how David included at his royal table a relative of Jonathan named Mephiboseth, who was "crippled in his feet," becomes a beautiful metaphor/image to us of what God's heart is about. The message can address what it is to feel crippled in our barren lives and then to realize what it means to enjoy God's aggressive invitation to the table of life.
Enhancement Ideas	This is the first of two weeks spent with the biblical character Mephiboseth. In this first week the main graphic can be that of a beautifully written personal dinner invitation to Mephiboseth. In a coordinating color print identical invitations for everyone attending worship. During the prayer time invite worshipers to write their name on their invitation. Then encourage them to keep that invitation in a place where they would be reminded of their ongoing place at God's table.
Featured Option	Baptism and Membership

Worship Celebration

Play preselected CD until service time

Opening Music

Guitar and Vocal
Light band

The Feast

Call To Worship

Host

"The Invitation"

House lights down to 50 percent; use visuals; soft music under

It's the banquet of the century and you're invited. Your name's been carefully engraved on the embossed invitation. You've been instructed to enter through the grand gateway. A valet parks your car while you slip into the gathering room for a refreshing, cool drink. Laughter and music fill the air as together with others you are drawn into the dining room. The table before you promises a feast that signals your taste buds into a mouth-watering frenzy.

A closer look at the grand display of tableware reveals a personal touch. Your name, your full name handwritten on a placard placed to reserve a seat for you. Just for you. Welcome to the table. Welcome to God's table.

Hear the words from Psalm 23.

> You serve me a six-course dinner right in front of my enemies.
> You revive my drooping head; my cup brims with blessing.
>
> Your beauty and love chase after me every day of my life.
> I'm back home in the house of GOD for the rest of my life.
> (from Psalm 23, *The Message*)

Will you join me now as we stand together and enjoy the presence of the one who sets the table?

God's Invitation

Song Celebration

Band

Platform and instrumental light sets; house lights back up; project words; band & choir exit following

Only Your Love
How Priceless

Membership and Baptism

Pastor-led
Soft music under

Prayer

Host
Continue with lighting, music, etc. Host calls for ushers after prayer

Lord, thank you for the priceless treasure of your presence here with us. Thank you that week after week, day after day, you extend the invitation to each of us to experience the reality of a relationship with you, the living God, here where we live.

Father God, for many reasons we haven't always felt welcome, whether in a church building, in a social setting, sometimes in our own families. Yet your love is extended without conditions. You don't post "no smoking" signs or insist that we clean up our act before we come to you. You are the very definition of love and all you ask is that we respond, that we get in a place where we can feel that love down to our very toes.

We want to know and experience the undeserved acceptance you offer. Thank you for your patience as we respond. Amen.

Offering and Featured Music

Lead singer/soloist
Light band; project main graphic

The Gift

Top Ten List

Host   "The RSVP"

Use breaking glass or other sharp, sudden sound effects between reading of items on list; project top ten list on screen

The RSVP
or TOP 10 EXCUSES FOR NOT WANTING TO EAT DINNER WITH GOD

10. Not sure if you could justify the meal as a legitimate business expense.

9. You thought RSVP meant Really Super Vulgar Person.

8. Jenny Craig advised against it.

7. You're listed in "Who's Not Who In Religious Circles."

6. You've never been sure what that little fork's for anyway.

5. You're lactose intolerant.

4. You suffer from poor conversational skills. . . . . "so . . . who do you think will win the Super Bowl?" (like God doesn't already know!)

3. (*Continuing with those awkward conversational moments*) "Did I say I didn't like the weather? Eleven degrees is my favorite temperature!"

2. Who would say grace?

1. (And the #1 excuse for not wanting to eat dinner with God . . .) Three words: I'm not worthy! I'm not worthy!

Insert Wayne and Garth video clip from "Wayne's World"

The real reason we hold back is that we don't feel worthy. Sometimes it's just easier to make excuses to cover up. But God invites us all to come to the table regardless of where we've been or who we are.

Storytelling

Drama player/storyteller   Mephiboseth (ad lib from 2 Samuel)

Light drama area; use crutch and table setting visuals

God's Invitation

Pastor
Light sermon set

Message

"Lame"

Band

Exit Music/Invitation

My Life Is In Your Hands
(by Kathy Tricoli)

Light front stage right / be prepared to extend music if necessary and play after send-out

Celebration Two

Longing for Belonging

Felt Need	Belonging
Desired Outcome	To become confident of our place in God's family
Theme	Mephibosheth/ Longing for Belonging
Word	2 Samuel 9:13
Metaphor/Image	A place setting at a beautifully set table
Synopsis	While the first week with Mephiboseth addressed our need for love, this celebration and message deal more specifically with our desire for acceptance into a group, a place of belonging. The message speaks about Jesus radically redefining acceptance and who can now sit at God's table. We become dramatically changed as we stay at the table and learn to accept ourselves and others unconditionally.
Enhancement Ideas	The drama set becomes the "living altar" for this celebration; it should be a simple table in a school cafeteria or pizza shop with numerous stools for players. The main graphic once again pictures a beautifully set table.

Worship Celebration

Opening Music

Vocalist

My Place In This World
(by Michael W. Smith)

Light and project vocalist; begin with instrumental only and conclude with vocal on chorus

Drama #1

8 players, teens dressed as young school children   "The Cafeteria"

Begin with cafeteria visual and sound effects throughout (no dialogue or microphones); lights up on drama area; project players; lights and sound effects fade when players freeze

The two wordless dramatic pieces are done in a similar fashion with the same eight teens and same basic set of tables and benches. In the first drama the teens are dressed as early elementary school children (a picture of school is projected on the screen). All have a sack lunch except one shy girl who has a lunch box. The other seven share fun, secrets, and laughs. They all have similar drinks, chips, etc. The one shy girl never quite fits in; she has a thermos, no chips, etc. Through their actions and gestures, it is obvious the other kids are not including her. As the bell rings at the end, all run out with the shy girl trailing at a distance.

Call To Worship

Host
Soft music under

We all remember the first time we realized life could be painful. In fact, we never really stop looking for a place to belong. Today we have come together to be honest about our need, to unmask deception and to consider that place God has designed just for us. Hear these words as spoken in the New Testament:

I ask . . . the God of our Master, Jesus Christ, the God of glory—to make you intelligent and discerning in knowing him personally, your eyes focused and clear, so that you can see exactly what it is he is calling you to do, grasp the immensity of this glorious way of life he has for Christians, oh, the utter extravagance of his work in us who trust him—endless energy, boundless strength! (Ephesians 1, *The Message*)

Let's begin this evening/morning by standing to sing together.

Song Celebration

Band
Come Into This House
Light band; project words; band leader seats afterward

Drama #2

Same players as above
"The Party"
Project pizza restaurant visual; light drama area; fade lights when players exit (one remains); band plays softly under this piece and then segues into featured music

The second drama is much like the first, yet the teens are older now and inside a pizza place (exterior projected on screen). Now the behavior is more sophisticated, yet every bit as hurtful. No one really wants to sit close to the shy girl; in fact, the boys even pull her seat out from under her. At the end, as the instrumental music begins to play "Everybody Hurts," the girl, now left alone by the others, puts her head down while the vocalist begins to sing. Lights fade on girl. She exits when the song is finished.

Featured Music

Band with lead
Everybody Hurts
Light band
(by R.E.M.)

Prayer

Host
Light extension and continue through next segment

Let's pray together.

Lord, as the song reminds us, everybody hurts. No one escapes the inevitable realization that to live in a broken world means to feel that brokeness at one time or another. To grow up in a fragmented culture is to know what it is to feel disconnected from ourselves, from others, from you.

Lord, we need your presence. Today we come to see in you eyes warm with understanding, to feel your arms extended in forgiveness and to hear your words spoken in acceptance.

As we remain with our heads bowed, let's hear and receive these words of hope and promise.

Words of Promise

Host, along with same 8 players
Host calls for ushers following this; soft music under

You groped your way through that murk once, but no longer. You're out in the open now. The bright light of Christ makes your way plain (Ephesians 5).

God rescued us from dead-end alleys. . . . He's set us up in the kingdom of the Son he loves so much (Colossians 1, *The Message*).

Since the One who saves and those who are saved have a common origin, Jesus doesn't hesitate to treat them as family (Hebrews 2, *The Message*).

But you are the ones chosen by God, . . . God's instruments to do his work and speak out for him, to tell others of the night-and-day difference he made for you—from nothing to something, from rejected to accepted (1 Peter 2, *The Message*).

You were lost sheep with no idea who you were or where you were going. Now you're named and kept for good by the Shepherd of your souls (1 Peter 2, *The Message*).

What marvelous love the Father has extended to us! Just look at it—we're called children of God! (1 John 3, *The Message*).

"For surely I know the plans I have for you," says the LORD, "plans for your welfare and not for harm, to give you a future with hope" (Jeremiah 29:11, NRSV).

We celebrate being part of his family and give out of our resources as an expression of thanks. Will the ushers please come forward at this time to receive his tithes and our offerings.

Offering/Featured Music

Vocalist
Visuals on screen; light grand piano

My Place In This World

Message

Pastor
Including video piece on "Reunions"; light sermon area*

"Longing for Belonging"

Closing Song

Band
Slowly light on band

Come Into This House

*This video that we produced asked ten people if they attend high school class reunions and why or why not. It brought us in touch with past pain.

To Life!
A Communion Celebration

Felt Need	To experience all the life we can
Desired Outcome	A commitment to drinking Christ's cup of joy and suffering, to experience all of life
Theme	To Life
Word	Isaiah 55:1-3
Metaphor/Image	Communion cup with a handle, more like a toasting mug
Synopsis	As humans we want to experience all that life has to offer. Many times that desire causes us to experiment with destructive behaviors. God's antidote is for us to drink the cup of Christ and thereby experience, in the midst of the good, the bad, and the ugly that life has to offer, all the fullness that God gives us. The celebration includes worship, laughter, and deep communion.
Enhancement Ideas	Strive to make this communion truly a celebration of our communion with Christ. Allow the culmination to be an actual toast—"To Life"—at the close of the celebration; thus, the metaphor becomes communion cups for everyone. Use the kind of cups with handles that everyone can clang together in a huge toast "to life."
Featured Option	Communion Celebration

Worship Celebration

Band
Light band

Opening Music

Celebration
(by Kool and the Gang)

Two Hosts
House lights down to 50 percent; no graphic; host asks congregation to stand

Call To Worship

Host I   (*reading from his or her Bible*) "Come, all you who are thirsty, come to the waters" (Isaiah 55:1, NIV).

We come today to lift up our cups, to celebrate life. All of life; the good, the bad, and the ugly.

(*Host I begins to clear his throat and continue this until Host II rushes up with a drink for him.*)

Host I   Thanks friend.

Host II   No problem. Just take all you need.

Host I   Well, uh, no thanks. I'll just hang on to it.

Host II   No thanks? I come all the way up here to rescue you and offer you this drink and you say "no thanks."

Host I   Well I've always been a little . . . choosy. And I don't know what's really in there.

Host II   Man, I've seen it all now.

Host I   Well Host II, I didn't see where you got this from. You could've put almost anything in here.

Host II   OK Host I, have it your way. Someday you might have to risk taking a drink someone else offers to find *real* life. (turns to audience) Oops, there I go preaching again.

Host I   Let's stand and begin our worship together.

24

Song Celebration

Band
Light band; host seats for "I Want To Know You"; project words

Great Is the Lord
I Want To Know You

Prayer

Host
Soft music under; main graphic remains but without words

Let's pray together.

Lord, we come to you today thankful that you have invited us to share your table. When we draw close to you, we catch glimpses of your deep love for us. It causes us to want to stay at your table and to get to know you. We want to know you more, to experience and taste the very life of God in our own human lives.

Lord, forgive our moments of reluctance. Forgive our passive ways that preclude us from actively participating at the table with you. Help us to be honest with ourselves and with you about how much of your life we are willing to embrace.

Lord, you have been there for us. When we've been hungry for life, you've given us bread. When we've been thirsty and tired, you've offered the cup. You alone give us life and provide purpose for each day, and we thank you. Because of Jesus, Amen.

Song Reprise

Band
Revert to song celebration lighting; project words

I Want To Know You

Offering/Mission Video

Host
Host calls for ushers first, followed by Mission video, then back to Host; light for speaking parts (see script); drama player will interrupt Host

Host I   As we continue our worship, we must honestly admit that we all share a certain reluctance in actually drinking from the cup of life that we are offered. *(Host I is beginning to have throat problems again and Host II will interrupt Host I to speak.)*

Host II   OK Host I. You've had your chance. I'll let you go get your own drink now and we'll cut straight to the point. *Host I graciously(?) exits.*

Top Ten List

1 Speaker (adult male)   "Bad Beverage Experiences"
Project Top Ten List items one at a time

And now, from the home office, the Top Ten Bad Beverage Experiences You May Have Had!

10. You've sighted UFOs: Unidentified Floating Objects.

9. You accidently drank shampoo as a child and your parents threatened to send you off to the Lawrence Welk Show.

8. You once had breakfast at Tiffany's and casually ordered Ovaltine.

7. Last Thanksgiving you overheard Grandpa insist that he left his dentures soaking in a cup just like yours.

6. You're afraid of being called "That Guzzler Formerly Known As 'Prince.' "

5. The snow your kid brought in to make slushies was a suspicious color.

4. You thought Alka Seltzer was the original spritzer.

3. You ordered that new "McMetamusil" shake and asked for it to be supersized.

2. Up until last year you thought cappuccino was one of the bad guys from *The Godfather*.

1. One word: Backwash. Need I say more?

To Life! A Communion Celebration

Pastor
Light sermon set

Message

"To Life"

Pastor-led

Communion

Band
Light altar and band; project main graphic

Featured Music

Hope Set High
(by Amy Grant)

Speaker leads

Raising the Cup

Band

Exit Music

Celebration

Happiness: What's Your Equation?

Felt Need	To feel happiness and joy in our lives
Desired Outcome	To understand that God alone creates our happiness/joy
Theme	Happiness: What's Your Equation?
Word	Genesis 29:31-35
Metaphor/Image	Smiley face; God + ? = ☺
Synopsis	We all have our own, often unspoken, formulas for personal happiness. We play on that reality in this celebration and strive to identify our own personal "happiness equations" while being challenged that only life in God can create true happiness and joy.
Enhancement Ideas	This celebration is a lot of fun. It uses simple math formula-type graphics and the well-known smiley face that represents happiness. On the altar place black and yellow smiley face fabric with candles and small chalkboards displaying math problems. The Call To Worship can be presented by a host communicating as a school teacher complete with a classroom pointing stick.

Worship Celebration

Opening Video

On the Street*
House lights at fifty percent; begin at service time

"What Makes You Happy?"

Featured Music

Band with female lead
Light band; house lights back up

If It Makes You Happy
(by Sheryl Crow)

Call To Worship

Host

"What Would It Take?"

Band moves into place at this time; introduce main graphic; Worship Host comes up to center stage after featured music piece

So very much of our energy each day goes into something we're going to call happiness. You may use a different word—fulfillment, success, or something else—but we all strive for happiness.

What's your equation? What would it take to make you happy? Our presence here today indicates that God is definitely one part of our equation for happiness.

For most of us, however, our energies say something else is in the equation too. Let's study what that looks like.

click remote; project equation

$$\text{GOD} + \underline{\hspace{3cm}} = \underline{\hspace{3cm}}$$

Now, I don't really know what's in your equation, but I can present the possibilities.

29

click remote; project equation

GOD + My Family = Happiness?

Number one, God plus my family. As long as the family is running in smooth order, no major conflicts and everybody's healthy, I'm happy.

Click remote; project equation

GOD + My Car = Happiness?

GOD + My Boat = Happiness?

GOD + My House = Happiness?

GOD + My Income = Happiness?

Number two, God plus my car, boat, or house. In other words, don't take my toys or my security and I'll be just fine, thank you. In fact, I think when my income reaches a certain level, all this stuff will be guaranteed—along with my happiness.

click remote; project equation

GOD + My Significant Relationship = Happiness?

Number three. This one rates very high. Shall we call it that "significant relationship?" It may not have actually happened yet, but someday I hope it will and I will do everything in my power to make it so. And if my "other" isn't significant enough, well then I'll change him or her. Or find a new mate. It's all in the equation.

Host walks back to front of stage to address audience.

We come here to remind ourselves of that one and only thing that we can truly count on. Let's stand together to sing and celebrate God's presence today.

Song Celebration

Band   Only Your Love

Vocalists and choir come up as song begins; light band and choir; project words; all stand to sing "Only Your Love"

Words Of Promise

Host
Continue with main graphic; soft music under until "Amen"

The freest person of all is the one who realizes that God is all-sufficient. Hear God's words of promise to us:

Whatever I have, wherever I am, I can make it through anything in the One who makes me who I am (Philippians 4, *The Message*).

"You're blessed when you're content with just who you are—no more, no less. That's the moment you find yourselves proud owners of everything that can't be bought.
"You're blessed when you've worked up a good appetite for God. He's food and drink in the best meal you'll ever eat" (Matthew 5, *The Message*).

Steep your life in God-reality, God-initiative, God-provisions. Don't worry about missing out. You'll find all your everyday human concerns will be met (Matthew 6, *The Message*). Amen.

Announcements

Host
Segue to mission video

Mission Moment Video

House lights at fifty percent; light for Host to call for ushers

Offering

Choir with lead   In This House
Light choir; no visual; choir exits following

Message

Speaker
Sermon light set

"What's Your Equation?"

Drama (within message)

Two young adult females
Light drama area; house lights down; fade drama lighting at end

"Leah Updated"

"Leah" Updated

Lights up on a young woman (Leigh) sitting reading a magazine in a doctor's office waiting room. A second young woman (Erin) approaches the scene, looks around for a place to sit, and approaches Leigh.

Erin   Anyone sitting here?

Leigh   Just me and little what's his name (*patting her belly*). We take up a lot of room these days. You might as well sit down. I think it's gonna be a long wait today. He had a delivery. Of all the nerve! Having a baby at nine o'clock on a business day! (*looks Erin over*) First baby?

Erin   Yeah. How could you tell?

Leigh   Well, you look rested, you've obviously had time to do your nails, and your purse wouldn't hold diapers and wipe n' dipes. How's that?

Erin   Pretty good!(*they laugh*) My name's Erin.

Leigh   I'm Leigh.

Erin   Do you have kids?

Leigh   Oh yeah. Veteran Mom. Yeah, I do kids real well. Boys actually. I don't think I've ever actually put my maternity clothes away in five years. It's been an ongoing blur of bottles, booties, and bibs.

Erin   Wow. I don't think I'll ever get there. You seem pretty together for having your fourth baby. Your husband must be really supportive.

Leigh   Mmmmm.

Erin   (*continuing on*) I'm on my own. I've decided to raise my baby by myself.

Leigh   Oh . . . well, I can relate to being by myself. I have a husband but he's, well, preoccupied.

Erin   Oh, yeah, I know that deal. The "go-to-work-come-home-watch-TV-go-to-bed" type?

Leigh   No, no. That would actually be easier to deal with. No, I guess the best way to say it is that he's always had someone else on his mind.

Erin   (*taken aback*) Oh. That's a tough one. Why do you put up with that?

Leigh   It's always been painful. He wanted to marry her in the first place but I think her dad kept them apart. We met and I loved him. A lot. Sort of a marriage of convenience. I put absolutely everything I had into making it work. I kept thinking once we started our family he'd forget about her. Now, three boys later I think he loves the boys, but me, well . . . We're still married, but I'm pretty sure his mind is somewhere else.

Erin   But you're pregnant again. How can you go through it all again alone?

Leigh   You know what? I'm not alone. Not any more. I got some help and I made a decision. For me. I'm putting my life together with the help of God, with or without my husband. No more bitterness eating me up. No more waking up each day hoping Jack will decide he loves me after all. That's not living, no matter how you slice it.

Erin   It seems like you should be entitled to a *little* bitterness. Do you even know this "person of his dreams"?

Leigh: Yeah, I do. I know her pretty well.

Erin   Oh, wow. She isn't a good friend of yours or anything, is she?

Leigh   (*slowly and sadly*) No, not really a friend; she's my sister.

fade lights

Closing Song

Band

Light band; project words

Let Your Healing Love

Closing Words

Host

Continue with music and main graphic

This video used our standard "On the Street" format. We go to a busy city location and interview people, asking each the same question.

Celebration Five

Outside the Lines

Felt Need   To discover our personal potential

Desired Outcome   To be challenged beyond our perceived limitations

Theme   Coloring Outside the Lines

Word   Ephesians 3:20-21

Metaphor/Image   Coloring-book page with coloring outside the lines

Synopsis   Going beyond the norm is a reoccurring theme at
                             Ginghamsburg Church. In this celebration we com-
                             municate that we must each embrace our unique-
                             ness and accept the challenge to go beyond
                             whatever limitations constrain us. "Coloring Out-
                             side the Lines" becomes a metaphor everyone can
                             understand and relate to.

Enhancement Ideas   Coloring books and crayons are good enhancement
                             on the altar for this particular celebration. On the
                             drama wing place an old-fashioned school desk
                             and bulletin board, helping the congregation
                             remember the first time they colored outside the
                             lines.

Worship Celebration

Band
Light band

Opening Music

Instrumental

Drama

One boy, about twelve years old,
a Charlie-Brown-type character

"Charlie Colors Outside the Lines"

Lower house lights; light drama area; project graphic; watch sound effects cues; band in place

Charlie	What am I doing here? Realistically speaking, this day is yet another step in my endeavor to become an integrated member of humankind. (*gets out crayons and paper*) I think I'll embark on my coloring project; a little red here, a touch of brown over here . . .
Teacher	(*heard from offstage*) Wah wah waah wah waah
Charlie	Yes ma'am. . . . What am I doing? Why, I'm coloring my picture for the science project.
Teacher	Wah wah waah wah waah
Charlie	Yes Ma'am, it's the sort of thing I can do to gain confidence and self-esteem.
Teacher	Wah wah waah wah waah
Charlie	Excuse me? My coloring? I'm using all of my favorite colors. The brown is really the best, don't you think? (*holds up crayon and paper for her to see*)
Teacher	Wah wah waah wah waah
Charlie	What? I'm doing it all wrong? I need to stay inside the lines? I'm afraid I don't see the lines ma'am. I see trees and frogs and wide-open spaces. I guess I failed miserably.
Teacher	Wah wah waah wah waah
Charlie	(*to audience*) It's not so much that I oppose conformity but that I'm never quite sure how to achieve it.

Music and lights down

Featured Music

Band

Like a Child
(by Jars of Clay)

Light band; house lights up; project graphic

Call To Worship

Host

Maintain graphic; no music; host asks congregation to stand

Children naturally color outside the lines until someone tells them it's not OK. This has been going on for a long time. Even back in Bible times we know the situations would have been much the same. Let me tell you about several "Famous Parental Admonitions" you may have missed seeing in your Bible.

"Moses, Momma said go around the puddle, not through it. Some day that puddle could be very, very deep and then you'll really be all wet."

"Sam? Oh Samson! You've got to get that hair cut. Someday you'll grow up and need a real job and nobody's gonna need a guy who looks like a hippie."

"Davey! Put that sling shot down and do something constructive, for heaven's sake!"

"Peter, don't you dare go in the pool without your water wings. You're just not ready to swim by yourself."

"Jesus! Slow down! Give that hammer a rest once in awhile! We're building a simple house here, not a mansion!"

We've all gotten used to hearing "Stick with the program or you'll never amount to anything!" We come here today to get closer to a God who tells us that real life may indeed be encountered outside the lines. Hear Jesus' words to us:

"There are no 'ifs' among believers. Anything can happen" (Mark 9, *The Message*).

"The person who trusts me will not only do what I'm doing but even greater things" (John 14, *The Message*).

Stand with me now as we affirm the One who challenges us to go beyond our own limitations.

Song Celebration

Band   I Waited for the Lord on High
Light band; project words; watch for leading vocalists to solo   Blessed Be the Name of the Lord

Prayer/Announcements

Host
Maintain graphic; light extension; host seats congregation after prayer

Father, we stop today to look up and recognize your greatness. You alone give us life and breath and freedom to go beyond the confines of our own limited reach.

Lord, thank you for the diversity of people here in this room and the opportunity we have to remind one another of what it means to each to be a representation of your artistic imagination. Thank you that you dared to color outside the lines when you created each one of us. Thank you for signing your name on our hearts, messy as they might appear. We are humbled to call you Creator and Lord. In Jesus' name, Amen.

Mission Moment

Video
House lights at fifty percent

Offering/Featured Music

Band with male lead   Still Haven't Found What I'm Looking For
                                                                    (by U2)

Band continues with same vocalists; light band; use graphic when appropriate

Outside the Lines

Message and Closing Words

"Outside the Lines"

Pastor
Light sermon area

Closing Music

Like a Child

Band
Continue lighting; same graphic as when sung at beginning of service

The Choice: A Communion Celebration for Lent

Felt Need	To identify with a higher power
Desired Outcome	To make a decision to choose Christ's path.
Theme	The Choice
Word	Mark 1:16-19
Metaphor/Image	A forked road
Synopsis	Part of how we define ourselves is by the decisions we make every day. Choices are important, and it is when we are faced with a clear choice and choose to follow Christ's path that we know our faith is at work. The metaphor of a fork in the road helps us to identify our need to choose Christ's path.
Enhancement Ideas	A forked road graphic and modern-day road maps strewn on the altar table set the scene for the theme. In a lighthearted manner the brief opening sketch reiterates how difficult it can be to make good road decisions while under stress. "The Road to Zion" is a great song to help us process the message.
Featured Option	Communion Celebration

Worship Celebration

Band
Light band

Opening Music

Instrumental

Host
Project graphic

Call To Worship

The journey continues. As we take the road to Easter, we are confronted with choices. Avoiding a choice is really to choose; no decision is really not an option. Maybe this will look familiar.

Drama

2 players, a married couple

"Where Do We Get Off?"

Project highway video; light center stage when players are seated; blackout at end

Harry and Margaret are traveling on the expressway on their way to a friend's home. Harry is driving and Margaret is navigating.

Harry	Margaret, nobody decides they don't know where they're going after getting on the freeway. I thought you had the directions.
Margaret	I do. Sort of. In my head. Let me see *(she squints her eyes to see ahead)*; three more streets up and turn left. Yeah. That's it.
Harry	Margaret. You can't turn left off the expressway. You mean get off at the third exit?
Margaret	*(looking uneasy)* Yeah. The third exit. Or the fourth. Let me see; I'll check the map.

41

Harry   Oh, that'll be a big help.

Margaret   Let's see . . . hmmmmm . . .

Harry   Margaret, the map's upside down.

Margaret   Oh, sure. I should have seen the airplane was belly-up. Here it is. Take the green road up about half an inch and turn left around the blue road.

Harry   *(exasperated)* Margaret, forget the map . . . Why is everyone crowding into my lane all of a sudden! Geez! *(He swerves to the next lane.)*

Margaret   Harry! Quit swerving! I can't stand it when you swerve like that!

Harry   Trust me Margaret! You need to trust me. What have I ever done to make you doubt my driving abilities?

Margaret, who is wearing a neck brace, turns slowly and glares with anger and disbelief at Harry.

Harry   Oookay!!

Margaret   *(looking back to the road)* Harry! This is it! This is the exit I remember that restaurant.

Harry   *(trying to get over to the right but the guy next to him won't let him in)* What's this guy's problem anyway? He won't let me over. What's he trying to say?

Margaret   I'm not sure, but he seems to know sign language real well. *(looking back at the road and getting almost hysterical)* Harry! We need to make a decision here! I think this really is our exit! We're going to miss our exit!

Harry slams on the brakes and bring the car to an abrupt stop on the highway (with sound effects).

Video stops to a stilled image

Margaret   *(thoughtfully)* Harry, I don't think that was one of the choices.

Harry throws his hands in the air in disgust. Margaret looks straight ahead. Blackout and begin song immediately

Song Celebration

Band
Light band; project words

Take Up Your Cross

Prayer

Host
Lower back lights to fifty percent; retain worship graphic; soft music under

Lord, you never said that to choose you was to choose safety or surety. Your gesture to offer us the choice of life was costly, risky. You gave up a son to make new life possible for us. Now you lay a challenge before us: To take up our cross and follow, to choose this day whom we will serve.

Lord, we believe; help our unbelief. We are enticed by your invitation but cautious to show commitment. Many of us are hanging out at the fork in the road and the only sign we see is the one saying "No Loitering. Make a decision and move on."

Yet, you do not ask that we travel alone. You promise the very breath and strength we need to make it every day. You prepare the way for us. You offer companionship.

Help us today, Lord, to be sensitive to your call, to be honest about where we are and to courageously make our choice. Thank you for the passion you've shown toward us. Through Jesus, Amen.

Song Celebration (continued)

Band
Lighting and word projection as before

What a Friend

Announcements/Offering

Host
Use graphic

Band
Light band; project worship graphic

Featured Music

Road to Zion
(by Petra)

Speaker
Light sermon area

Message

"The Choice"

Pastor-led
Band
Light altar; light band

Communion

Road to Zion

Closing Words
Host invites congregation to say closing words together
Print words in bulletin or project

I choose to follow Christ's path. I won't give up, shut up, let up until I have stayed up, stored up, prayed up for the cause of Christ. I am a disciple of Jesus. I must go until he comes, give until I drop, preach until I know, and work until he stops me. And when he comes for his own, he will have no problem recognizing me. I belong to him.

Host

Go this week and choose your path. Amen.

Band
Light band; project worship graphic

Music Reprise

Take Up Your Cross

Jesus Now: A Lenten Celebration

Felt Need

To know God's living presence in our lives

Desired Outcome

To experience renewal and awareness of the daily presence of Christ in us

Theme

Jesus *Now*

Word

Luke 24:13-16; John 16:13-16; Ephesians 1:17-19

Metaphor/Image

Old flannel graph/Bible figures

Synopsis

Faith must be relevant in the here and now. Without recognizing our methods and habits as outdated and stale, we often plod through life trying to keep the flannel graph Jesus of our childhood meaningful to our lives today. This celebration addresses the fresh presence of Christ among us each day.

Enhancement Ideas

Nothing seems to give the impression of old-fashioned, outdated faith quite like the flannel graph biblical characters we used as children. Using these images for graphics, play up the fact that these flannel graph figures are one dimensional and lack the living breath of God that is needed each day. Also work with clichés to further press the point that faith goes past trite sayings to practicing the daily presence of Christ.

Worship Celebration

Opening Music

Choir with male lead

I Am Not Ashamed

With music track; light choir; choir exits following

Call To Worship

Host

"Present Tense, Please"

Band in place; project graphic

What would a messiah born 2000 years ago look like in today's world? Try as we may, one of the most challenging exercises is to picture Jesus in the here and now. Early Sunday school memories may actually detract from our efforts, for he was usually rendered in lifeless flannel-board scenes

Project flannel-board scenes at points marked by asterisk

*There he is teaching!

*That's him holding a lamb.

*Now he's talking with a Samaritan woman and look,

*another conversation with a man named Nicodemus.

The closest thing to action came

*when the disciples in their miniature sailboats bobbed across the blue flannel board sea. I remember one scene of Jesus standing in the temple with a whip in his hand, but it matched nothing else I had learned about him. I certainly never saw him at a party. I may have learned facts about Jesus' life in Sunday school, but as a person he was remote and two dimensional. Past tense.

As we continue on our Lenten journey, our greatest longing is to know God in the here and now. Day by day. Present tense. You may remember this great song that expressed that desire.

Song Celebration

Band

Light band; project words

Day By Day
I Waited for the Lord On High

Dialogue

Host

Host steps back but stays on stage following

"Tired of Clichés"

Clichés can be a handy form of communication. They allow us to speak more, think less. Clichés create clever little islands of understanding. I mean, in no uncertain terms and all thing being equal, I could make a long story short and like a bolt out of the blue and in one fell swoop coin a phrase and hit the spot hook, line and sinker. I could say we're packed in here like sardines but the more the merrier, so let's put our best foot forward, pass the plate, and put our money where our mouth is. After all, the buck stops here! Just food for thought.

Actually, clichés get tiring and monotonous. Perhaps God feels the same way in listening to us . . .

Reader's Theater

Reader

Continue lighting; old-fashioned organ chords under; quick blackout at end

"Tired of Clichés" (continued)

I come to the garden alone, while the dew is still on the rose.
But I'm struggling now to update this somehow,
and find God before we both start to doze.

It's not that I don't want to talk to you, or "get the victory," or "pray it through."
Its just that the lingo confuses me so, the words we repeat from so long ago,
I struggle to know just what I should say besides "Thank you Lord for this beautiful
    day."

I mean, you really are "great" and you really are "good,"
but I can't seem to say things like others tell me I should.

48

I hear "Bless Johnny and Janie and Susie and Rob,"
But my mind is screaming out "What About Bob?"
What about people who just don't get blessed; is that a sign that you love them less?

And then there was Grandpa; I loved him a lot.
I heard "God called him home" and I had the thought
that God had "called" enough people to that heaven of his,
so why "call" the grandpa of a five-year-old kid?

We say things like "saved" or "don't worry, trust the Lord."
We ask for "traveling mercies" and "God bless our food."
Yet I can't help but think as I'm sitting here now
that you want to exist here, alive and somehow
more a part of my life than I can now see.
A presence, a passion, inside of me.

Sweet hour of prayer, sweet hour of prayer, it calls me from a world of care.
But I wonder as I'm alone with you, is it just an hour you've called me to?

Prayer

Host
Soft music under ("Open Our Eyes"); begin words when Host says "Amen"

Religious jargon and tired phrases may not be God's idea after all. We need to find ways to realize God's presence fresh and new each day. Let's take a moment to pray silently and be honest and open before God. As we bow our heads, use one or two sentences to tell God what's going on inside of you. Be open to God's presence as you deal with the things that concern you most. Confess your need for God's life to invade yours in new ways, in the present tense.

Pause to allow for personal prayer time

Lord, we all need to learn to talk with you heart to heart. We need to get past the clichés, past the worn-out and familiar, and into real-life conversations that tell you who we really are and ask you to show yourself to us. You've created us to enjoy change and newness, yet in our walk with you we tend to slip back into the old and familiar. We shift into automatic rather than experience your presence as fresh and new each day. Show us a better way Lord. Amen.

Song Celebration

Band   Open Our Eyes
Light band; project words

Mission Moment

Video
House lights down; still at end

Follow Up /Offering

Host

This is where our money goes in accomplishing the mission of Jesus. As individual lives are strengthened, the entire body of Christ is renewed. As the body of Christ we want to resource and support that kind of activity. Will the ushers come now to receive the gifts we've brought to share?

Featured Music

Band with vocalist   I'll Lead You Home
Light band/ project graphic for enhancement   (by Michael W. Smith)

Message

Speaker   "Jesus Now"
Light sermon area; three persons from audience will read scripture at various times during sermon

Closing Music

Band with vocalist

Light band; project enhanced worship graphic

Breathe In Me
(by Michael W. Smith)

Closing Words

Host

Life isn't a two dimensional flannel-board story. Life is about what Jesus is doing now with you. Listen, ask, trust, and experience the real thing. Amen.

Exit Music

Band

Light band; project band

Day By Day

Journey of the Heart: A Lenten Celebration

Felt Need

To be totally real and open about who we are: Authenticity

Desired Outcome

To open our hearts and allow God to heal us

Theme

Cleaning Up: Journey of the Heart

Word

Luke 4:1-13

Metaphor/Image

Messy closets

Synopsis

The season of Lent is a season of preparation. We are reminded that the closets of our hearts must be cleaned and swept anew and that in our culture, closets can be places of hiding. Addictions and control issues may lurk in the closets of our hearts. We address the issue using a combination of humorous drama, music, and the message.

Enhancement Ideas

A great graphic is a simple closet with the door slightly ajar. Further drive the metaphor on the stage in the drama "The Simptoms," a parody of the popular television cartoon. The drama set can reinforce the theme with a large yellow closet.

Journey of the Heart: A Lenten Celebration

Worship Celebration

Opening Music

Instrumental

Band
Light band; project band

Call To Worship

Host
Project closet graphic; band in place

Today: "Messy Closets and the People Who Own Them"

You walk to the end of the hall and face it. The closet. The dreaded closet. One little peek inside and you rediscover a mess bigger than life itself. It only takes you three seconds to decide to:

1. Thoroughly plunge in and organize it
2. Compulsively scrub up and sanitize it
3. Remember your neighbor's nightmare garage and thoughtfully rationalize it, or
4. Close that door, turn around and forget you ever saw it.

Jesus had the knack for seeing deep into the closet of the heart and confronting sin head-on. His words to those who struggled were, "Do you want to be well?" Do you? Do you want to clean out your closet?

We come to dare to open our closets and to invite God's healing presence inside.

Song Celebration

Where Do I Go?
Seek First
(from "Songs From the Loft")

Band
Light band; project words

Prayer

Host

Host seats congregation first; band realigns for featured music; continue with closet graphic

Let's pray together.

We come here, Lord, to look inside, deeper inside than we are totally comfortable with. It's tough to be honest. We fear the truth that might be discovered and wonder what we'll do with the mess. We don't really know if we have what it takes to be authentic inside and out. As we continue this Lenten journey, give us strength and courage to face what may be in the closet. Thank you for the promise of your presence, the promise of real life for all who dare to come clean. You felt so strongly about this that you gave your very life to make it possible. We thank you. Amen.

After prayer

Thinking about your own home, chances are you have at least one messy closet in the house. But maybe the mess is really just a *symptom* . . .

Drama

Four players (the Simpton family)   "The Simptoms"

*Lower house lights; theme music and graphic until Martha **stands** to speak (see script); Repeat theme music at end*

Henry and Martha enter stage right to couch. Barry and Liz enter stage left. A pillow fight ensues before Martha settles it and Barry and Liz are squeezed off the couch onto the floor. Henry uses the remote control to flick on the imaginary TV, and Barry and Liz prepare to watch also.

Martha   All right everyone. Today's the day. We have to clean out this closet. Everyone helps or nobody goes anywhere today.

Barry   Ooooooo! Liz! You wouldn't want to miss your book study at the library. They might read a page without you. They might read a chapter without you. I'm getting scared!

Liz   You're just jealous because my IQ is a three digit number!

Barry   What? 911?

Martha   OK, OK. Save it for later.

Henry   Way to break it up there Martha. *(To kids)* Listen to your mother. *(He switches stations with the remote control and the kids are again interested in the TV.)*

Martha   Now Henry, you're in on this too. Everybody's got stuff in here. *(She slowly opens the closet door.)* Lots of stuff! *(She pulls out a string of things and happens upon several empty donut boxes.)* Henry, what's this? What in the world are all these empty donut boxes doing here? I don't remember buying all these donuts! *(Henry jumps up to confiscate the boxes, embarrassed he's been found out.)*

Henry   Doh!

Liz   Not Doh, Dad, donuts. Mom found where you keep your stash.

Barry   Way to go Mom! You scored big time.

Henry   AHHHH! Can't a man even keep a little comfort on the side? *(grabs the boxes and stuffs them into a trash bag)* Whatever happened to the king of the castle?

Liz   This isn't the fifties, and we live in a modest housing development. *(getting up off the floor)* Mom's right. Let's get this closet cleaned out and organized. Studies prove that cleaning out the closet can be simultaneous with cleaning out the mind.

Barry   Count me out.

Liz   Not so fast oh "brother of my youth." What exactly is this? *(holding up his last report card)* Hmmmm, Barry Simptom, Homeroom 238. Let's see; *(opening it)* Math: D; Social Studies: D; Earth Science: D; Behavioral Science: F+.

Martha   F+? How do you get an F+?

Barry   I flunked but I worked very hard at it.

Liz   Right. Classic Underachiever. Why do you even get up in the morning? What is your overall contribution to society?

Barry   *(seriously)* I'm mostly here to irritate annoying females and to provide a role model for immature adolescents everywhere.

Liz   Don't flatter yourself!

Henry   *(jumping up to join in picking through the garbage)* Martha, what are all these?

Martha   *(embarrassed and rushing over to grab the books Henry has found)* What? Well, uh, well, they're my books. My little library.

Henry   Little library! When do you possibly have time to read all these? I thought you cleaned house and made dinner all day. Martha, are you dabbling in romance novels? Are you seeking fulfillment outside of our relationship through the printed page?

Martha   *(collapsing on the couch, upset and crying)* At first it was just little cartoons in the paper. Then it was a quick glance at the book covers and titles in the display at the grocery next to the produce section. Soon I bought my first novel and before I knew it, I was hooked. I buy one a week. I'm, I'm sorry. *(burying her head and sobbing)*

Liz   Well, it looks like the closet cleaning is directly propelling us toward knowledge of who we really are. An embarrassing and shameful account of our lives as we'd rather not know them. A mortifying elucidation of deprivation.

Barry   *(sarcastically)* That worries me too.

Henry   Let's just quit here and now. We'll throw all this stuff back in to the closet and pretend it never happened. *(beginning to put things back into the closet)*

Martha   That's quite a good idea Henry. I think the sun just came out and we could work out in the yard instead. *(wholeheartedly helping Henry)*

Barry   You won't get an argument out of me. I plan to begin target practice with the Flannigans' cat. *(pulling the slingshot out of his pocket)* It has a white spot in the back of its head.

Liz   You mean you're all just going to walk out of here and ignore the mess in the closet? Everyone's just going to go their separate ways and allow this secret garbage to putrefy?

Barry   Sure we are. Don't have a cow man.

Blackout

Mission Moment

Video
Host transitions; house lights remain lowered

Offering/Featured Music

Band with male lead
Light band; project worship graphic

Don't Look Away
(by Gary Adrian)

Message

Speaker
Light sermon area; scriptures read intermittently from the floor

"Journey of the Heart"

Closing Song

Two vocalists
Light vocalists; project illuminated closet graphic

There's Freedom In You
(by Gary Adrian)

Closing Words

Host

The journey of the heart isn't a comfort trip but there is healing along the way. Open that closet door and choose the real life he offers. Amen.

Exit Music

Band
Light band; project worship graphic

Where Do I Go?

Following From a Distance: A Palm Sunday Celebration

Felt Need	To identify whom to follow in life
Desired Outcome	To identify closely with Jesus, despite the risk involved
Theme	Following From a Distance
Word	Luke 9:23
Metaphor/Image	A fire/smoke among some rocks
Synopsis	This was a Palm Sunday celebration. We expand on Peter's fear of totally identifying with Jesus and draw a parallel between Peter's not wanting to get too close to the fire (Jesus) and our reluctance to take a stand as followers. We too often prefer to follow from a distance, standing outside the fire.
Enhancement Ideas	The graphic for this celebration has a fire-charged look. The altar table could have numerous candles placed closely together as if to give the appearance of a fire. The drama wing is staged for the modern-day retelling of Peter's denial through the eyes of a diner waitress. The Garth Brooks' song "Standing Outside the Fire" nails the theme.

Worship Celebration

Opening Music

Band

Light band; project band

Instrumental

Call To Worship

Host

Project worship graphic; vocalists in place

Palm Sunday.

The Lenten journey continues, this time on the final path toward Jerusalem, carefully chosen palm branches paving the way for the Master.

To be there in person was to have to choose.

To choose how close to get to him.
To choose how many hosannas to shout in his favor.
To choose how long to stay awake in the garden.
To choose how much money to take in return for your soul.
To choose how close to get to the fire before the rooster crows and you realize it's just too hot.

We settle for the safety of following from a distance rather than get burned. Yet we come here today to risk being right up in the center of activity. To choose the place right next to Jesus. Let's begin our worship celebration together.

Song Celebration

Band

Project words; band leader asks congregation to stand and be seated when appropriate

Hymn Medley
I Love You Lord

Host
unscripted

Prayer

Band
Light band; project words

Song Reprise

I Love You Lord

Video
House lights down

Mission Moment

Host
House lights back up

Follow-Up/Offering

Band
Project words; band exits following

Song Celebration (continued)

I Worship You

Monologue

Female adult   *"If You Can't Take the Heat"*

Lower house lights; light drama area when speaker in place

My mama always said any girl of hers should know how to make a livin.' I don't s'pose she meant I'd be a waitress my whole life, but, well, it's a good job and the tips aren't bad, and, hey, I've learned a lot. Not about books and that sort of thing, but a lot about people. What's in 'em. What makes 'em tick.

Let me tell you about what happened last Thursday workin' the night shift. It was a weird sort of night. A lot had gone on that day to make a person feel a little uncertain. My boss had taken the evening off to do some "community business." I think he was in on gettin' a guy arrested for disturbing the peace. I knew the man they arrested. He had a funny first name; Jesus. He'd been a customer of mine several times. Never really hurt anybody but made guys like my boss uneasy. Bad for business I guess.

Anyway, one of this guy's friends comes into the restaurant late that night lookin' real tired and alone. He asked for a table close to the fireplace. Everybody likes those seats—till they figure out how hot it gets up there.

He was a nice lookin' guy, big. I knew he'd be hungry but when I went to take his order he just wanted coffee. He was nervous and jittery. When he looked up to speak to me, I saw eyes that I knew I'd seen before. His look scared me. "You're a friend of that guy they arrested today, aren't ya?" I said. "I've seen you two in here together several times."

He looked down at the table and wadded his napkin up in his fist. "I don't even know his name," he said real low and heavy-like.

Scared me, cause I knew I was right about him! Three guys sittin' at one of my tables close by noticed him too. One hollered out "Hey Pete!" (His name was on his shirt.) "How's come they got your friend and not you?" He just shot back, "Stuff it buddy. I ain't who you think I am."

He brooded a while. I filled his cup a few times but couldn't get no conversation out of him. Pretty soon he tossed some change on the table, stood up, and walked over to the cashier. She recognized him too.

"Was you part of his group? That guy that was taken in for disturbin' the peace? I saw you together yesterday."

He says, "Lady, I don't know what you're talkin' about" He was real edgy. I felt nervous watchin' him. The chimes from the church across the road rang to break the awkward silence. Twice. Two a.m.

He hurried out, shiverin' as he walked further and further from his place by the fire. It shakes you up to see grown men cry.

Fade lights

Speaker
Light sermon area

Message

"Following From a Distance"

Band
Light band/ project worship graphic

Featured Music

Standing Outside the Fire
(by Garth Brooks)

Host
Continue to project graphic

Closing Words

The call of Jesus goes way beyond believing. Don't settle for following at a distance. Dare to smell like smoke. Amen.

Band
Light band; graphic remains

Exit Music

Standing Outside the Fire

Celebration Ten

Living the Unexplainable: An Easter Celebration

Felt Need	Possibilization
Desired Outcome	To find renewed hope that we can live fuller lives out of the faith that we have
Theme	Living the Unexplainable: An Alternative Look at Easter
Word	Luke 24:11-12
Metaphor/Image	Empty grave clothes, rolled strips of cloth, one candle
Synopsis	This Easter celebration was a an innovative twist on the message of Easter. Realizing that our culture is currently intrigued by the paranormal, we rediscover the amazingly unexplainable events of Jesus' death and resurrection. This celebration also explores the possibilities the Resurrection introduces: "If God can do this, what else can God do?"
Enhancement Ideas	This celebration allows for a very real and alternative look for Easter. No eggs, no colorful flowers; instead, consider the stark look of large rocks placed on the altar with rolled muslin strips, candles, and a thorny crown among the rocks. The prayer can be enhanced by pictures of new life in many forms, which give us hope for small resurrections in our own lives. In addition, make use of the drama "The Easter Files" using characters similar to those in the popular television show "The X Files." The entire progression powerfully leads to the exciting message of hope "Living the Unexplainable."

Easter Worship Celebration

Opening Music

Band (no vocal)   Christ the Lord Is Risen
Choir comes up during opening music; no graphic

Call To Worship

Host
With "tomb" graphics; no music; invitation to stand

Easter provides us with the one question we cannot ignore: What do you do with an empty tomb? What do we do when we search the cave only to find the doorway wide open, the grave clothes lying disheveled to the side, and only the faint smell of spices hanging in the air?

Just like everything else in Jesus' life, the Resurrection evoked contrasting responses from those who encountered it. For some, the missing body confirmed the doubts they'd had all along—just another hoax or another fanatic with some magic up his sleeve.

Yet for others, for those who by faith followed this phenomenon all the way, the Resurrection was the first in a long string of miracles that would change their lives forever. Easter became the preview of ultimate reality. Death is reversible. He is alive.

Let's stand and sing.

Song Celebration

Band   Christ the Lord Is Risen
With words projected; band leader seats congregation following   (UMH, # 302)
Choir   Crown Him With Many Crowns
With two-three leads and live accompaniment; no graphics;   (Michael W. Smith, "I'll Lead You Home")
choir exits following
Band   He Is Lord
With words projected   (UMH, # 177)

Prayer

Host
Continue with soft music under; lower house lights

The older we get, the more difficult it becomes to believe in a God who does resurrections. We grow up and experience the limitations of life and the pain of death. Eventually we decide it's really hard to live out of wonderment. It's easier to live out of doubt.

Begin visual graphics

And yet, every once in awhile, a fresh glimpse of the miraculous catches our attention. Little "aftershocks" of God's creative energy break out and attempt to rekindle the wonderment. How do you explain these everyday miracles?

Continue graphics with one graphic remaining as a still shot to end of prayer

We see God's hand, and the thought occurs that if God can do this, God can give us life. God can use that same skill and power to work in the difficult places in our lives; in broken relationships, in dreams gone sour, in families in strife, in hopes deeply buried.

Death is reversible. God recreates life. As we go to God in a time of prayer, let's take a few moments to silently be in God's presence. Let's open ourselves up and listen to God's desire for our miracle.

Pause for silent prayer

Thank you, Lord. There is no other one we can talk to in this way. You are Lord. You do resurrections on a daily basis. Rekindle our sense of wonder.

Song Reprise

Band
With words projected

He Is Lord

Welcome/Offering

Host
Project "tomb" graphic and continue to end of "Liquid"; band rearranges

Many times the aftershock of an earthquake exhibits as much energy as the earthquake itself. Each year we celebrate the aftershock of the resurrection of Jesus. We come together to once again affirm that he is Lord. Today we want to extend a warm welcome to those of you for whom this is your first time in this place. Make yourselves comfortable; we want you to feel at home.

Now as we enjoy this time of music and reflection, will the ushers come forward to receive the offerings we've brought to give?

Featured Music

Band
Continue with "tomb" graphic

Liquid
(by Jars of Clay)

Drama

Two players
House lights down; backdrop in place; theme music and graphic introduction; bring in music again toward the end, then fade out; fade lights at end

"The Easter Files"

The Easter Files:
A Case For Belief

The setting is Agent Max Mullins's office, subbasement of FBI headquarters, Washington D.C. Mullins is engrossed in a file and texts on his desk. He seems rather frustrated. (Begin with music and graphics. Mullins enters. Fade music slowly, bring lights up after Mullins is seated.)

Enter Agent Deborah Tully. She is dressed in professional business attire. They wear badges, guns, etc. Mullins looks up as Tully enters.

Mullins	Tully.
Tully	You wanted to talk?
Mullins	Yeah, shut the door.
Tully	OK, what's the big conspiracy this time? *(She pours herself some coffee.)*
Mullins	Ha ha. Actually, I may have stumbled onto something big. Very big. And the funny thing is, it's been right under my nose all this time. It's actually something you may have been right about.
Tully	Oh? Well now I am intrigued. Should I sit down for this?
Mullins	You may want to. *(She sits.)*
Mullins	Do you remember about a month ago when we were investigating the strange downing of Flight 240 in Utah?
Tully	Yes, we determined a water fowl got sucked into one of the engines, causing it to crash. I guess you could say it was another one of your wild goose chases.
Mullins	I guess. But that wasn't the important part.
Tully	No? It wasn't—exactly a baffling case. An unfortunate occurrence between humankind and nature.
Mullins	Yes, well the last night we were there, I finally picked up and read something in my hotel room that I've never taken very seriously.
Tully	The instructions for the TV remote?
Mullins	No, I'm talking some heavy stuff here. Even bigger than that.
Tully	I'm not surprised.
Mullins	Honestly Tully, this thing has really thrown me for a loop. You know this whole time I never regarded it more than some ordinary, customary part of tradition.
Tully	Mullins, what are you talking about?

Mullins	Small, green, in every hotel room, found by Rocky Raccoon? The Gideon's Bible?
Tully	Mullins, I'm impressed. So what's the big discovery?
Mullins	Absolute truth. Possible. There are some questions here we've been ignoring like they were just some kind of Sunday school class.
Tully	What questions?
Mullins	Evidence for the reliability of the Scripture, Jesus' actual resurrection from the dead, evidence of miracles Jesus and his disciples performed, even astronomical proofs for the existence of God.
Tully	Proof and evidence. That's quite a step for you Mullins.
Mullins	Hey, everybody makes improvements.
Tully	Mullins, are you sure of what you're talking about? I've never heard you talk like this before.
Mullins	True, but that's only because I've ignored the blatantly obvious for so long.
Tully	Which is?
Mullins	That thing that even Pascal proclaimed: that we all have a God-sized vacuum inside of us. I'm drawn to this stuff. I think I want to believe. The more I look into this, the harder it is to shake.
Tully	This is too weird. I can almost take all your conspiracies and UFOs and unexplainable disappearances, but I'm afraid your walking out a bit far on this one.
Mullins	Where's your faith Tully?
Tully	I'm talking about you.
Mullins	I know, so am I.
Tully	Gee. I thought you had made some big discovery.
Mullins	I'm getting to that.

Tully   So what else have you found out?

Mullins   Miracles. Jesus' miracles.

Tully   Yeah?

Mullins   You admit that we have seen some pretty amazing and unexplainable things.

Tully   I believe we've seen some rather unusual aspects of science and nature that don't always occur on an everyday basis.

Mullins   OK then, how do you explain miracles? Weren't they performed to convince nonbelievers?

Tully   Maybe.

Mullins   The Resurrection. Big, big deal right? But why?

Tully   I agree Mullins. I think it was a supernatural event.

Mullins   OK, but if it did not actually happen then really all of life is for nothing. If the foundation of Christianity is a lie or a fabrication from the first century, and Jesus wasn't God, then the basis for Christianity is false. If he really did rise from the dead, then this is the most important discovery I've ever made. I mean, evidence about the inability of farmers and fisherman to overpower highly trained guards at Jesus' tomb, the paying off of the guards to lie about Jesus' body being stolen, and more evidence is beginning to shed new light on my previous doubts.

Tully   Mullins, I just don't know what to say. I feel like I need a sixth sense here. And you. What are you going to do about this x-file?

Music in; fade lights; fade music after exit

Speaker
Light sermon area

Message
"Living the Unexplainable"

Closing Words

Host
Project original "tomb" graphic, then use closing graphic and freeze

The tomb is empty and now we decide. If we want to experience the phenomenon, we must choose to live out of the side of faith. Amen.

Exit Music

Band   Liquid
Continue with graphic ("to be continued . . .")

The Move: Where Do I Go From Here?

Felt Need	To dream new possibilities for our lives
Desired Outcome	To take a step in faith despite our fear of letting go
Theme	Abraham: Where Do I Go From Here?
Word	Genesis 12 and 13
Metaphor/Image	Boxes, moving van
Synopsis	As we explore the unsettling feelings of a moving day, we are able to identify with Abraham and Sarah when they decided to give it all up and go for God's promise. It is easy to forget that biblical personalities experienced the same apprehensions that we do now. Faith takes us all to potentially uncomfortable places.
Enhancement Ideas	In a twist of creativity, set up the metaphor in the church parking lot by placing a rental moving trailer just outside the front doors. On the platform place a montage of packing boxes, loose items, and a chair that can collectively double as the set for the modern-day Abraham monologue.

Worship Celebration

Band
Light band; project band

Opening Music

Where Do I Go?

Host
Project truck graphic

Call To Worship

"Moving Day Blues"

Moving Day. What could be more fun? The whole experience ranks right up there with root canals and remodeling. Actually nobody likes moving because it's about leaving everything that's familiar and secure to go after the unknown and uncomfortable. It's physically and emotionally draining to say the least.

In the Bible's book of Genesis we're told that God wanted to do something very big in Abraham's life but there was one prerequisite. Abraham would have to gather up his family and move. He'd have to pack up lock, stock, and barrel and leave the familiar in order to discover the phenomenal.

Today we come together to look at the next move. To discover where we go from here and to listen to the one who wants to show us the way. Let's stand together now.

Band
Light band/ project words/ band leader seats us

Song Celebration

Almighty
Trust and Obey
(UMH, #467)
Seek First

The Move: Where Do I Go From Here?

Video
House lights down; begin video as soon as last song is finished

Mission Moment

Host
House lights up

Announcements/Offering

Band
Light band/ globe graphic

Featured Music

I Believe In You
(by Bob Dylan)

Male Adult
House lights down; light drama area

Drama

"The Move"
(Copyright © 1997 by Rich Swingle
Used by permission)

Prop List:
Phone that rings (not portable)
Two answering machines
Lots of clothes, shoes, ties, jackets, etc.
Table lamp (fairly large)
A box large enough to pack the lamp
Garbage can (large enough to fit the lamp)
A chair that swivels
Newspapers (several)
Small purse

Abe rises from behind a large box. He is reluctantly packing a table lamp into the box. He begins crumpling paper and wadding it into the box. He sees an article from the hometown paper and sets it aside. Phone rings. It is muffled. Abe scrambles all over trying to find where the phone has been hidden.

Abe	"Honey! Where'd we put the phone?" (*He finally finds it inside a ski cap.*)

Abe	"Oops! I was making sure it would fit in a ski cap for safe travel. I guess it does."

The answering machine begins. Abe picks up the phone, but it's too late and the machine will not cut off. Abe begins searching frantically for the machine.

Answering Machine	(*Abe's voice; muffled, but audible*) You've reached the Davidsons. We're away from the phone right now, probably out making last minute arrangements for the big move. (*Frantic*) Pray for us! (*Calm*) I don't know how we're going to get everything done in time, but I'm sure it will all come together. Leave a message and we'll get back to you as soon as we're able.

Abe	I'm so sorry, I'll get that turned off. Packing and everything we just don't know where a thing is. (*Muffling the receiver; To Sarah*) What about the machine? The answering machine. Do you know where it is? (*He finds it wrapped in a sweater. He looks guilty. He clicks it off.*)

Abe	(*Into phone*) "It was in a sweater. Lou! Where are you?"

Abe sits in a swivel chair and swivels positions to become Lou.

LOU	"Abe, listen. I just don't think I'm up for this. I don't mean packing, Abe, I mean the whole business. I was just watching a talk show from New York. We don't want to go there. They had these people calling in who had been assaulted. Gobs of them, Abe. One was mugged on his way out of a Knicks game. The host said he should have expected it since the game let out late. Another was stabbed with a screwdriver in broad daylight. The host told him he should have known better than to make eye contact with a stranger on the streets of New York. Another caller was doused with gasoline, set on fire, and pushed off the roof of his own building. The host told him that living in New York you just have to expect that kind of thing from time to time.

74

Yes it was on TV.

A talk show, I tell you.

Well actually it was a "Saturday Night Live" sketch, but they wouldn't make jokes like that if they weren't based on truth.

And let me tell you, running a deli out here and running a soup kitchen in New York are two very different things.

Oh, look, Abe, I know I've committed. I've committed, I'm going, but if you change your mind . . .

I hate call waiting. You get back to me fast, Abe, do you hear me?"

He swivels to become Officer Duff.

Officer
Duff   "Hello, Abe? This is Officer Duff.

No, there's no trouble. Unless there's something you need to tell me?

I'm just pullin' your leg, Abe. Actually the guys down here at the station wanted me to call and let you know we're sorry to hear you're moving out. Your deli's always been more than a respectable establishment and . . . oh, I don't want to get all sappy on you here. We just wanted to give you a going away present as a token of our appreciation of all you've done for the community.

A bullet-proof vest.

You're going to need it, Abe. I have a cousin who's on the NYPD. He found a fellow with his pants down around his ankles on a subway platform. Some muggers pulled his drawers down in the scuffle so he couldn't run after them. Awful.

Well, no, I guess the vest wouldn't be of much use for a situation like that, but it'll keep out bullets, knives, and any other sharp objects. I hear scissors are the weapons of choice for junior high schoolers these days.

Oh, come on Abe. It's the least we can do.

Well, if you change your mind, let me know.

75

He swivels to become Lou.

Lou   "What, did you switch carriers?

So, I'm telling you, if you change your mind I will be the first to support you. Anyhow, I'll see you tomorrow.

Tomorrow, I tell you. I've got to go in for all my shots this afternoon.

I know it's not Mozambique, but they've got people from over a hundred nations living in that city. Who knows what creepies are crawling around out there.

Oh, you and your call waiting. I'm hanging up. I'll talk to you tomorrow."

He swivels to become Aunt Edith.

Aunt Edith: "Abe? This is your Aunt Edith. Have you changed your mind yet?

Don't you leave this town, darling. We need you. What are we going to do without our dear Davidson Deli. You know the new owner wants to turn it into a burger joint and name it after his daughter: Cow Patty's it's going to be called. Disgusting.

Stay, darling. Redeem the deli.

Oh, you are so hard headed.

I got you something, dear. Here, listen."

Aunt Edith holds a body alarm up to the receiver and clicks it on and then quickly off.

Aunt Edith   "It's a personal alarm, Sweet Pea. If anyone who looks suspicious heads in your direction just flip this sweetheart on and he'll run for cover. And it has a special feature for Sarah. She can keep it in her purse and attach the string to her belt loop. Then if someone runs up from behind and steals her purse it'll keep screaming at him until he drops it."

She is "demonstrating." The string won't come loose.

76

Aunt Edith   It's advertised to work this way.

The string comes loose and the bag goes careening across the floor. She races after it, dropping the receiver behind her. She grabs the bag and re-inserts the pin. She picks up the receiver.

Aunt Edith   "It works.

Abe, are you still there? Abe, Honey?

Oh, I'm sorry, but just think of how that robber's ear is going to feel.

Okay, Darling. All the best to you. Drop me post cards along the way. And let me know how that alarm works out.

Aren't you glad now that you don't have kids to worry about?

Bye bye.

He swivels to become Abe. He's rubbing his ear. He hands up the phone and goes back to packing.

Abe   Honey, I don't know, maybe I didn't hear God right. Maybe we just should stay here, start a soup kitchen for the derelicts here: all three of them."

The phone rings again. Abe stares at it. It rings three times. On the fourth ring he leaps for it.

Abe   Hello?

Mr. Goddard. Hi.

We're getting there. Listen, I, uh, Sarah and I both, and Lou, have been thinking that, uh, maybe we should just uh (*He looks back to Sarah, then up to heaven*) bring some of our own machines from our deli.

Well it looks like we'll have room."

He pulls the lamp out of the box and places it in the garbage can.

Abe   Need anything? Just an extra two pounds of faith.

Thank you.

We'll see you soon.

He hangs up.
Lights down.

Speaker
Light sermon area

Message

"Where Do I Go From Here?"

Band
Light center stage; project globe graphic

Closing Song

Choose Your Tomorrow
(by Tamara Batarseh; sung a cappella)
Love in the Real World
e-mail: [love@abel.telalink.nets
to check for music availability]

Host

Closing Words

Band
Light band; project globe graphic

Exit Music

I Believe In You

Celebration Twelve

God's Green Light

Felt Need	To explore all the possibilities our lives can offer
Desired Outcome	To move out in faith because of God's promises to us
Theme	God's Green Light
Word	Acts 3
Metaphor/Image	Traffic signs/stoplights
Synopsis	Most people think of God as the ultimate nay-sayer; but truly God is the God of "yes, go!" In this celebration we explore our own tendencies to be red lights of negativity in others' lives. We also realize God's permission, God's green light, that enables us to move out with the faith we have.
Enhancement Ideas	Place various street signs all around the sanctuary and platform. The main visual can be a real stoplight purchased secondhand and wired with a remote control. Use the different light colors (red, yellow, green) to emphasize the messages spoken throughout the celebration.

Worship Celebration

Opening Music

Band
Light band; project video of signs

Signs
(by Tesla)

Call To Worship
Project sign graphic; stoplight on drama wing will flash

Do this; don't do that! Can't you read the signs? Signs—they tell us what to do, where to go, and how to get there.

If your life was a sign, what would the sign say? In the great traffic light of life, what color are you? Rules and regulations red? Fear-inducing yellow? Or are you a light of hope and health to others? Are you green light in a red light world?

We come together to speak words of faith so that we can then go out to be light to others. We stand now as affirmation of God's life-giving presence among us.

Song Celebration

Band
*Light band; choir enters at beginning; project words;
band leader seats congregation*

Lord I Lift Your Name On High
We Need Jesus
(by Petra)

Prayer

Host
Continue soft music under; project worship graphic; add words on cue

We live in a world of people who, just like us, need Jesus. Many long to hear good news. Many long to see green lights of hope.

All too often we've not been the presence of God to others—to our children, our spouses, friends, parents, coworkers. Rather than welcome, encourage, and affirm, we may have offended and excluded through our critical, negative, and judgmental attitudes.

As we pray silently now, take time for reflection and confession. Thinking over your life, be willing to ask forgiveness for the hurt your red-light attitudes may have caused.
Pause for a brief time of silent prayer

Now as we end this time of prayer, will you say the words that appear on the screen together with me as we join our hearts in confession.

Lord, hear the prayer of my heart. Forgive my shortsighted ways. Forgive me for speaking words of harm when I could be giving messages of love and acceptance to others. Help me to affirm your life-giving presence both in myself and in those around me. Amen.

Featured Music

Choir   Holy Is the Lord
No graphic; project choir

Mission Moment

Video
House lights down; begin immediately; choir exits

Host
Band ready for featured music

Follow-Up/Offering

Band
Light band; project band with sign stills

Featured Music

That's Just the Way It Is
(by Bruce Hornsby and the Range)

One male
Piano entrance and exit music then fade; light drama area after player is seated

Monologue

"Magic Legs"

"Magic Legs" / Everest Glump

Theme music begins immediately. Lights up on drama wing after Everest is seated. Music fades.

Mama always said you have to do the best with what you got, no matter how little it is. A little faith, a little love. Even I know about that.

Hello. My name is Everest. Everest Glump. People call me Everest Glump.

Those must be real comfortable shoes. Mama always said you could tell an awful lot about a person by their shoes; where they goin', where they been. I bet if I thought real hard I could remember my first pair of shoes. Mama said they'd take me anywhere. They were my magic shoes.

I remember the day they took me right down to the front steps of Beulah Baptist Church next to Piggly Wiggly in Greensboro, Alabama. That's in Greensboro County. I remember walkin' by and seein' this man sittin' there on the steps for no particular reason at all, except that he couldn't stand up and walk away 'cause his legs were as crooked as a politician. Which was a bad thing.

You wanna chocolate? You never know what you're gonna get in a box of chocolate. That man didn't know what he was gonna get that day. He didn't know that out of the blue clear sky two men would walk up those steps and give him a miracle.

God's Green Light

Course Mama always said miracles happen every day. Some people don't think so. But they do. These two men were named Peter and John and they had them a plan. It was a fine idea. When the man with the bad legs asked them for money, they said they didn't have any. Peter spoke up and said he'd just give him what he did have and just like that he reached down and grabbed that man and pulled him right up. Right then it was like God showed up and made his legs straight as an arrow. It gave people hope. He could run like the wind blows.

From that day on whenever that man was goin' somewhere he was running. He got him new legs. Magic legs. They'll take him anywhere.

And that's all I have to say about that.

Lights fade, theme music concludes

Speaker

Light sermon area; altar time at conclusion

Message

"God's Green Light"

Band

Light band; project band

Closing Music

We Need Jesus

Host

Closing Words

Never underestimate your ability to be God's "yes" for others. Give freely out of what you've been given. Go be God's green light. Amen.

Band

Light band; project worship graphic

Exit Music

Celebration
(by Kool and the Gang)

Breaking the Ball and Chain

Felt Need	To be free from our "stuck" places, the weights of our past
Desired Outcome	To articulate of our personal mission statements and serve freely
Theme	Breaking the ball and chain (of our stuckness)
Word	Matthew 28:16-20
Metaphor/Image	Ball and chain
Synopsis	Getting out of our stuck places is a common theme at Ginghamsburg Church. On this particular occasion we are speaking to the need we all have to write personal mission statements and then allowing God to set us free from any ball and chain that would hinder us from freely giving up our lives for Christ's kingdom.
Enhancement Ideas	Along with candles and fabric on the altar, display a large ball and chain (try a costume/party supply store) to help drive the theme. The "On the Street" videos always set up the theme provided that the right question is asked of those being interviewed.

Worship Celebration

Opening Music

Band with Choir

Light band and choir; project worship graphic

I Got the One I Want

(by Amy Grant, from "Songs From the Loft")

Video Clip

On the Street

House lights down; begin immediately

"What Holds You Back?"

(We asked: "What holds you back from doing what you really want to do with your life?")

Call To Worship

Host

Freeze and maintain final image, then go to worship graphic

You've got the want to, you've got the need; so what holds you back?

Each of us has been carefully designed with a unique purpose in mind, but life's obstacles have us convinced that we're not fit for the job. Invisible ball and chains hold us back from what we were created to do. Can you say, "Christian Couch Potato?"

Jesus had bigger ideas. He said, "The person who trusts me will not only do what I'm doing but even greater things, because I, on my way to the Father, am giving you the same work to do that I've been doing" (John 14, *The Message*).

We worship today to focus on God's voice and to be reminded that we are created to do great things, free from anything that would hold us back. Let's stand together.

Song Celebration

Band and Choir

I Will Call On the Lord
We Believe In God
(from "Songs From the Loft")

Light band and choir; project words; band leader seats congregation

Prayer

Host

Project images, change at points in script indicated by asterisk; soft music under ("We Believe in God")

* Where does God go through you? * Do you suppose that God would like to go places that we, being God's hands and feet, resist going? * Jesus said that inasmuch as we serve the most vulnerable among us, * we are serving him. *

Go to chain visual

So what holds you back? So many times it's the labels we put on ourselves that render us unfit for service. Labels like "recently divorced," "chronically ill," "partially educated," "painfully shy," "financially unstable." That jaded self-concept becomes an invisible ball and chain; it's like a dead weight, holding us back from real life.

As Christ's body of believers, will you join me as we confess the struggle within? Using the words that appear on the screen, let's speak the prayer of our hearts together.

Project words

Father, we believe that to go where you go is to find life. We know that to do your work is to find meaning in even the most mundane experiences. We want to be your hands and feet, to walk and serve your people.

Lord, forgive our human, limited thinking. Cause us to re-label ourselves in light of who you have created us to be. Set us free for your purpose. Amen.

Song Reprise

Band

We Believe In God

Continue lighting; project words

Breaking the Ball and Chain

Video
House lights down; vocalists and choir exit

Mission Moment

Host

Announcements/Offering

Band
Light band/ project worship graphic

Featured Music

Ball and Chain
(by Susan Ashton)

Speaker
Light sermon area

Message

"Breaking the Ball and Chain"

Speaker
Light extension; project worship graphic

Commitment/Closing

Band
Light band; project band

Exit Music

I Got the One I Want

Celebration Fourteen

Destination Known

Felt Need	To discover God's unique purpose for our lives
Desired Outcome	To realize the treasure of God's destiny for each of us and develop our life mission statements
Theme	Destination Known
Word	Acts 22:6-11
Metaphor/Image	Maps, a huge treasure chest
Synopsis	We often emphasize that God has created each of us with a unique purpose to be on earth, a given "destiny." As a way of "getting at" that destiny, we encourage followers to develop a life mission statement. By using the metaphor of hidden treasure, we develop this celebration in such a way as to help people become purposeful about identifying their own life mission statements.
Enhancement Ideas	So many segments enhance this theme, beginning with the popular tune "Show Me the Way" and followed by a film clip from "Goonies" in which the young characters are searching for hidden treasure. The drama sketch is a dialogue between two young adults regarding their futures but actually is the story of Esther and Paul, two biblical role models with their own destinies. Finally, inside the sermon experiment with a model of a live interview, the beginning of what we now refer to as "Stool Time."

Worship Celebration

Opening Music

Band
Light band; project map graphic

Show Me the Way
(by Styx)

Video Clip

From "Goonies"
House lights down

The boys find a map in the attic.

Call To Worship

Host
House lights back up; go from video to map graphic

You may not be up to just another crazy goonie adventure, but what if . . . ? What if the map really can show us the way?

The possibility of buried treasure could excite us as kids. Now as grown-up kids there can be no greater treasure for us than to find God's purpose for each of our lives. It's the destiny we're here to fulfill.

We come here to worship the God who chooses us and who has gone ahead of us to draw the map that leads to the treasure: our created destiny. Let's stand and sing.

Song Celebration

Band and Choir

Joyful, Joyful
(UMH, # 89)

Choir comes up at beginning; light choir and band; project words

Choir with male lead

We Declare Your Majesty

No projection; continue lighting as before with live instrumentation

Congregational Prayer

Host

Project words on screen; lower house lights; continue instrumental under

Lord, we declare your majesty. We see your power all around us. We believe. Help our unbelief. You have shown us the path of life, the map that we need. We confess we often choose a different direction or fail to choose at all. We sense the direction you desire but often get distracted along the way.

Thank you for new starts. Thank you for unfailing love that proves over and over again that you do not leave us alone. You are there for us. In your presence our joy is full. Amen.

Song Celebration

Band and Choir

We Exalt You

Project words; light band and choir

Announcements/Offering

Host

Featured Music

Band
Light band; project worship graphic

Treasure
(by Steven Curtis Chapman)

Storytelling/Drama

Two young players: one male, one female
Light drama area; house lights down

"Destination Known"

Two young adults are walking across the stage as though they are hiking, dressed in hiking gear and carrying a map.

Ben So, what do you want to do when you grow up?

Abby When I grow up? Thanks Ben.

Ben No I mean, I've been thinking a lot about this. I'd love to think I was here for a purpose. I've always wanted to be "called by God" for something really unique. I need a life-map.

Abby It could happen . . .

Ben *(sarcastic)* Yeah, like in fairy tales. But I'm here. And I don't know how to get there from here. Kind of like us right now—a little confused about where this trail goes. *(He looks at his map confused.)*

Abby So you want a map; like a cosmic flash of light.

Ben What?

Abby Like Paul. The Bible Paul. Acts 9. He's on his way to Damascus, anxious to get there to "knock off" Christians for God. He was passionate about it too. So Paul gets off at the Damascus exit and was literally blinded by a light blazing from the sky. It knocked him flat. Then he hears this voice say "Hey Paul! Why are you out to get me?" Can you say panic attack? After the voice identified itself as Jesus, Paul asks a very good question. "What do I do now?"

91

Ben   I can relate to that.

Abby   Turns out God was just getting his attention. Later God gave him back his eyesight and laid out Paul's life-map. He said that Paul was now supposed to tell everyone he saw about what he'd seen and heard. From that day on Paul knew exactly what he was supposed to do. How to use his passion. Every day, right at the top of the "to do" list was "tell others what I've seen and heard."

Ben   That's what I need all right. A flash of light. Maybe it's just a guy thing . . .

Abby   Could be, but, I guess I'd love to know what I'm supposed to do. What I'm good at.

Ben   Like "Esther the Beauty Queen, saving her people from death?"

Abby   What?

Ben   Esther. Bible stories aren't just for men anymore.

Abby   And Esther was good at . . . ?

Ben   Being in the right place at the right time mostly. As the story goes, the kingdom of Xerxes had this leader threatening to kill the Jews (not a new idea!) So this feisty little Jew named Mordecai positions his young cousin Esther to be in the King's top-level harem. Esther was awesomely beautiful.

Abby   Of course.

Ben   But she was Jewish too. So when the right time came, she used her beauty and favor with the King to beg for the lives of her people, which was actually against the law. King Xerxes could've had her blown away just for asking. Knowing that, Esther's attitude was, "If I die, I die." All or nothing. She just wanted to do what she was meant to do.

Abby   So did Xerxes kill her?

Ben   No. It's amazing. He basically said "Your wish is my command." He ended up promoting Esther and Mordecai to royalty status and empowering the Jews to defend themselves against anyone who would come against them. Not a bad ending.

Abby   For a Bible story. Or a fairy tale. If only it could happen that way today. Do you really think we're all here for a purpose? Is God still drawing individual life-maps?

Ben   Maybe. I don't know. What *do* you want to do when you grow up? Let's get going. *(They exit together, still trying to figure out the map directions.)*

Message

"Destination Known"

Speaker
Light sermon area

Closing Words

Speaker

Exit Music

Show Me the Way
(by Styx)

Band with vocalists
Light band; project worship graphic

93

Celebration Fifteen

Please Pass the Blessing: A Mother's Day Celebration

Felt Need	To be loved
Desired Outcome	To experience and know God's love, even in the absence of parental love
Theme	Please Pass the Blessing
Word	1 Samuel 1:21-22; Mark 10:13-16
Metaphor/Image	Parental hand on kid's shoulder
Synopsis	Mother's Day is one of the largest attended celebrations in our calendar year. However, we work hard to make every celebration of the year speak to seekers in all situations, so we expand the message of Mother's Day to issues that will hook all of us. In this service we address our common need for love and the hope of experiencing God's love and "blessing" even as adults.
Enhancement Ideas	It seems there is no better image of "the blessing" than a hand on a child's shoulder. Open this celebration instrumentally, then go to a humorous video clip making the point that a lot of us missed "the blessing." Amy Grant's song "The Power" communicates a strong message of love's importance. The mother-daughter drama brings up painful relationship issues that lead into the message "Please Pass the Blessing."
Featured Option	Infant Dedication/Baptism

Worship Celebration

Opening Music

Band   Instrumental
Light band

Call To Worship

Video Clip with Host   "The Perfect Home"
                                              from "Throw Mama from the Train"

Owen brings his mother's tea cup with trepidation. Instead of receiving it she knocks it across the room and yells at him.

House lights down for beginning; begin clip immediately following band; fade from "house" graphic to worship graphic; Host asks congregation to stand before song celebration

The Perfect Home. We all grew up there. Our families were our world. They could be the cause of our greatest pain, or the source of our greatest blessing. God's intention was that we would *bless* one another. Hear from God's Word:

> Mostly what God does is love you. Keep company with him and learn a life of love. . . . [Christ's] love was not cautious but extravagant. He didn't love in order to get something from us but to give everything of himself to us. Love like that (Ephesians 5, *The Message*).

We come today to find out more of what it means to freely give to others what Jesus has freely given to us—the blessing of God. Let's stand for worship now.

Song Celebration

Band   Blessed Be the Name
Light band; project words; house lights back up; band leader seats congregation following   Shine On Us

Infant Dedication/Baptism
Follow-Up/Prayer

Host
Continue soft music under; project worship graphic

Lord, you are the one who calls us. You began chasing us long before we were even aware.

Loving God, today we have come to bring these precious ones into your presence, to state what you have known all along—that they are indeed yours. Today these parents' desire to make it clear that they are caretakers, but you are owner. You create and sustain. You have woven plans of hope for your children of promise.

Lord, thank you for your mark on our lives. Thank you for your call that first accepts us as we are and then goes before us to show the way. You have given us significance. Thank you for shining on us today. Amen.

Announcements/Offering

Host

Featured Music

Band with female lead
Light band; project worship graphic; band exits following this

The Power
(by Amy Grant,
from "House of Love")

Drama

Two players   "All I Ever Wanted"

Lower house lights; light drama area as players enter; fade at end/ project players

All I Ever Wanted

Kitchen scene. Mother (M) is in kitchen gulping coffee and eating a roll while studying paperwork. She's in a hurry, checking her watch.

Lights up as daughter (D) enters.

D   Are you going somewhere? *(feeling out of the situation)*

M   *(not making eye contact)* Huh? Yeah. I've got to go back to the office for awhile. These reports are due tomorrow and I'm still on the rough drafts.

D   When do you think you'll be home? "Cause there's something . . .

M   *(still uninvolved in conversation and not really listening to D)* Honey, I don't have time to talk, I've really got to run. I'll be probably be back after you're asleep. Make sure your brother takes a shower tonight, OK?

D   *(starting to get agitated, but pacing herself)* Mom! Look there's something I've been working on and I kind of need to discuss it with you.

M   *(a brief look at D)* Sure, but can't we do this later? Your father is harping on me to get these bills done too, and I've just got a lot on my mind.

D   *(agitated)* But Mom . . .

M   *(hurried)* Look, make sure the dryer shuts off. It's been sticking.

D   *(more agitated)* Mom . . .

M   *(very short)* Carrie, I don't have time! *(She gathers her belongings and starts to exit.)*

D   *(firmly)* Mom, if you leave I won't be here when you get home!

M stops dead in her tracks, silence, turns slowly to D and says with amazement:

M	*(articulate and distinct)* What did you say to me?
D	*(softer this time, but assertive)* If you leave I won't be here when you get home. *(timidly but firmly)* I'm serious!
M	*(angry)* I did not raise my daughter to talk to me that way.
D	*(shoots back)* It's the only way to get your attention!

Now the fight begins.

M	What has gotten into you?
D	*(spiteful)* You have! You have gotten into me.
M	*(amazed)* What is that supposed to mean?
D	Mom, I'm sixteen and you still don't know I hate chocolate. You still think I read Judy Blume books and that I have no clue where babies come from, *or* that I *have* a boyfriend!
M	Where is all of this coming from?
D	*(sarcastic)* It shouldn't be a shock to you. *(pauses as she regains her calmness)* Look, I've really been feeling depressed lately and I really want to talk to someone, so . . . *(scared to tell the truth)* I went to see Mrs. Dirk in the guidance office. A few times now. *(Getting excited)* It's really been helpful to me. I've really started to understand a lot of things about myself. *(Confession-like)* I feel like a misfit, a complete failure. I don't have any close friends. I need to talk about this. I need you to know why I am the way I am.
M	*(confused)* To know what? *(louder and defensive—drilling)* Did someone hurt you? Have you not told me about someone? Someone I don't know? *(talking fast)* Tell me! I'll go and talk to Mrs. Dirk myself. No one is gonna hurt any of my children. They've got another think coming if . . .
D	*(interrupts abruptly)* Mom . . . it's you! You're the one hurting me.
M	*(speechless and sort of chuckling)* Me?

D   Yes. That's what I've been trying to tell you. *(getting upset and emotional)* Mom, you're never here and when you are you never have time for me. You've never spent any time getting to know *me*. Now I'm growing up and I can't seem to make friends. I fight with everyone, just like you and Dad. How can I make friends with complete strangers when my own mother is a stranger?

M is obviously uncomfortable and trying to brush the issues under the rug.

M   Carrie, you're making too much out of this. My mother wasn't exactly Mother Teresa but I got over it!

D   *(crying and semihysterical)* What is it gonna take? Am I going to have to die before you tell me you love me? *(She sits and tries to calm herself down.)*

M is angry and confused; dramatic pause; both try to regain composure.

M   I'm sorry you think I am such a failure. Maybe when you have kids of your own you'll understand. I hope your daughter thinks more of you than mine thinks of me.

D   *(gently and genuine)* There you go again Mom. Blaming it all on someone else so that you can get on with your life. I hope my daughter thinks a lot of me too, because I've made a decision that my life is going to be different. I want my children to know me and I want to know my children. *(tenderly)* Mom, I don't want it to be like this. All I ever wanted was for us to be friends. I want to sit down with you and talk about my future, my life. *(pause)* I need you. I love you. But I can't change you.

Lights fade

Speaker

Message

"Please Pass the Blessing"
from Forrest Gump

Light sermon area; Three video clips: 1. Forrest with his Mom; foot in grate. 2. Jenny returns to her childhood home, the scene of her abuse. She picks up rocks and throws them at the house, then breaks down crying. 3. A wheelchair-bound Lt. Dan sits in a dark hotel room lamenting his life circumstance to Forrest.

Host

Closing Words

Band
Light band; project worship graphic

Exit Music

The Power

The Language of Love: A Pentecost Celebration

Felt Need	To know real love in our lives: Authenticity
Desired Outcome	To give and receive love that creates "realness"
Theme	The Language of Love
Word	Acts 2:11-12
Metaphor/Image	The Velveteen Rabbit
Synopsis	Once in a while we hit on a felt need in our congregation that seems to warrant a second or third week in a theme. We typically create a new metaphor and present yet a different aspect of the theme, which in this week's case was "love." Using the metaphor of the children's storybook character "The Velveteen Rabbit," we describe how love, given and received, ultimately allows for our "realness" as humans.
Enhancement Ideas	Two songs by Celine Dion truly empower the theme of God's love and "realness." Interweaving the excerpted story of the Velveteen Rabbit (see drama) with a video our team composed of people reminiscing on their own first recollections of love drives the theme further. Along with the drama set of a nursery room including the rabbit himself, a favorite of this celebration could be the souvenir given to each person: a small patch of brown velvet to slip on their key chains to periodically remind them of God's love and their own "realness."
Featured Option	Communion Celebration

101

Worship Celebration

Band with female lead
Light band; project stills as scripted

Opening Music

The Power of Love
(by Huey Lewis and the News)

Three players
House lights down; light drama area

Drama

What Is Real?

What Is Real?

One woman is seated and two young girls snuggle in close to hear the story.

Woman   Now then, where were we in the story?

Girl 1   The boy found the Velveteen Rabbit in his Christmas stocking.

Girl 2   The rabbit was starting to feel lonely in the nursery.

Girl 1   Yeah. And the Skin Horse was the only one who was kind to him. The Skin Horse was old and wise and he understood nursery magic.

Woman   (*opening the book to settle in and begin reading*) "What is real?" asked the Rabbit one day when they were lying side by side near the nursery fender, before Nana came to tidy the room. "Does it mean having things that buzz inside you and a stick-out handle?"

"Real isn't how you are made," said the Skin Horse. "It's a thing that happens to you. When a child loves you for a long, long time, not just to play with, but really loves you, then you become Real."

The Language of Love: A Pentecost Celebration

"Does it hurt?" asked the Rabbit.

"Sometimes," said the Skin Horse, for he was always truthful. "When you are Real you don't mind being hurt."

"Does it happen all at once, like being wound up," he asked, "or bit by bit?"

"It doesn't happen all at once," said the Skin Horse. "You become. It takes a long time. That's why it doesn't happen often to people who break easily, or who have sharp edges, or who have to be carefully kept. Generally by the time you are Real, most of your hair has been loved off, and your eyes drop out and you get loose in your joints and very shabby. But these things don't matter at all, because once you are Real you can't be ugly, except to people who don't understand."

"I suppose *you* are Real?" said the Rabbit. And then he wished he had not said it, for he thought the Skin Horse might be sensitive. But the Skin Horse only smiled.

"The Boy's Uncle made me Real," he said. "That was a great many years ago; but once you are Real you can't become unreal again. It lasts for always."

The Rabbit sighed. He thought it would be a long time before this magic called Real happened to him. He longed to become Real, to know what it felt like.*

Lights fade.

Call To Worship

Host
Lights down on drama area; project worship graphic

Real isn't how you are made; it's a thing that happens to you. For centuries the church has celebrated Pentecost, the powerful entrance of the Holy Spirit into the lives of ordinary human beings. This weekend we celebrate Pentecost—the day that God empowers us to become Real through the gift of the Holy Spirit. Join me now as we stand to worship together.

*Excerpted from *The Velveteen Rabbit,* by Margery Williams Bianco (New York: Smithmark Publishing, 1996).

103

Song Celebration

Band

Only Your Love
We Need Jesus

Band leader has congregation stand for the first song; choir enters; lights up on band and choir; project words

Video

Lower house lights; continue soft music under

"When Did You First Feel God's Love?"

Prayer

Host

Light extension; continue with worship graphic and soft music

What is your earliest memory of a God who loved you? When did you first feel loved by God?

(*Insert personal story. For example:* For me it was an after-school club that my sister first discovered. Her fourth-grade teacher welcomed a group of us into her home to play and to learn about Jesus. It was a fun place; so warm, safe, and inviting. A great place to feel welcome and become Real.)

You know, none of us is here by accident. No one is here because of a program or a particular Sunday school lesson alone. Most of us have been loved into the Kingdom in one way or another by a *person*; a teacher, a friend, a parent, or a coworker willing to be the smile or touch of God on our behalf.

Let's bow for prayer and take a moment now to thank God for those people. Just where you are, say the name out loud of that person you are thankful for, the person that first helped you feel loved by God.

Pause for response

If we share the love of Jesus,
    see each other as he sees us,
    the world will know we all need Jesus.

Help us, Lord, to be the expression of your love to those for whom you care so deeply. Thank you for loving us first. Amen.

Song Reprise

Band and Choir

We Need Jesus

Light band and choir; project words

Choir

One Voice

Continue lighting; with female leads; trumpet solo

(from "Together for the Gospel")

Announcements/Offering

Host

Choir exits

Featured Music

Band with female lead

Because You Loved Me

Light band; project worship graphic

(by Celine Dion)

Message

Speaker

"The Language of Love"

Light sermon area

Communion

Pastor-led

Soft music under; light altar area

Closing Words

Host
Light drama area; project host

Real isn't how you are made. It's a thing that happens to you. When someone—God—loves you for a long, long time, not just to use you, but really loves you, then you become Real. Once you become Real you can love someone else in Jesus' name, and they can become Real too. Once someone is Real, they can't become unreal again. It lasts for always.

Take your patch home, put it on your key chain, and remember the day God made you Real. Amen.

Exit Music

Band
Light band

The Power of Love

The Presence:
A Communion Celebration

Felt Need	To experience the physical presence of God
Desired Outcome	To have an actual experience of God's love
Theme	The Presence
Word	Genesis 28:16-17
Metaphor/Image	Homemade bread and aroma
Synopsis	As our theme of love continued, this week we were determined to allow people to truly experience God's love through one of the five senses that we do not often consider: smell. One aroma that seems to say "love" is the smell of baking bread; hence, our metaphor. To allow for the actual presence of God to be "smelled" and thus "felt" is a way of ministering God's love to our people and sparking their interest for more.
Enhancement Ideas	Find a potent gingerbread (or other) potpourri oil to heat in a central, obscure place. Communion presents the opportunity to display huge loaves of homemade breads of varying hues and textures. Consider ending the celebration with an invitation to baptism while a vocalist sings "Because You Loved Me."
Featured Options	Communion, adult baptisms

Worship Celebration

Opening Music

Band
Choir and vocalists come up; light band only

Because You Loved Me
(by Celine Dion)

Call To Worship

Host
Project worship graphic on cue (see script)

The fragrant perfume of fresh flowers after a spring rain.
The sweet scent of a little child after a day of outdoor play.
Large loaves of bread, fresh out of the oven.

(*Insert a personal story. For example:* If I were to describe to you one of my favorite smells, I'd have to begin with the smell of my grandparents' home. It must've been the combination of my grandmother's hand lotion, my grandfather's aftershave, and a touch of the aroma of my grandma's great cooking mixed in. What a comforting scent. To this day if I smell anything like it, I can become teary-eyed with the memory of their presence.)

We come today to celebrate The Presence. The Presence of God. God's life broken for us to taste, smell, and see that God is good. Not a memory, but a reality. Not a scent confined to the walls of the church, but the awareness of God's aroma wherever we are. Let's worship now.

Song Celebration Medley

Band and Choir lead
*Light band and choir; project all words beginning **after** first solo*

Soloist asks congregation to stand after first solo and be seated after "Holy Ground"

Holy Ground
Holy, Holy, Holy
(UMH, # 64)
Surely the Presence
Sweet, Sweet Spirit

Prayer and Video Introduction

Host
Lower house lights

Lord God, surely your presence is in this place. Thank you for making this safe space, this holy ground where real life can grow. Amen.

Mission Moment

Video
Continue with house lights down

Announcements/Offering

Host

Exciting ministry happens as ordinary people give of their time and financial resources. As we put legs on the mission of Jesus, we are in turn blessed with knowing we've had a part in something that goes far beyond us. Let's enjoy the choir now as the ushers come to receive God' tithes and our offerings.

Featured Music

Choir with female lead   One Less Stone
Light choir; project choir; choir exits following

Monologue/Prayer

One player

Light stage when player is seated; project player

"The Presence of You"

The Presence of You

Dear God,

The world that I live in has been grey for so long, I've walked in a haze, my faith lacks a song.
The days are so busy, the years pass too soon. My senses are dulled, my heart's out of tune.
And I wonder out loud on the bleakest of days—Am I missing the presence of you?

A long time ago I said I believe, took in all the facts I could find to receive.
I learned all the verses, had it all in my head, even said prayers before going to bed.
Still I knew in my heart at the end of those days I was missing the presence of you.

They told me you lived here some years and then died, rose out of the tomb and before leaving you tried
to convince those who followed they would not be alone, that their lives you'd invade, your presence make known.
So I ask what happened that now I can't see—I am missing the presence of you.

Life has a way of numbing the senses, once pain has it's day we put up our defenses.
I can't see your face, I can't touch the wind. I can't smell your presence when the air is so thin.
And the deepest place in my heart wants to know, to experience the presence of you.

I don't need a system, a rulebook, a plan. I need the presence of you, the touch of your hand.
The scent of your life so close to my own, the taste of your goodness, the words "you're not alone."
To experience you on my good days and bad, dear God show me the presence of you.

The Presence: A Communion Celebration

Speaker
Light sermon area

Message

"The Presence"

Pastor-led

Communion

Band
Light band and altar

Song Celebration Medley

Speaker
Project worship graphic; soft music under

Closing Words/Baptisms

Band with female lead
Continue with graphic and lighting

Exit Music

Because You Loved Me

Passing the Presence: A Father's Day Celebration

Felt Need	To know God's presence in our lives
Desired Outcome	To be challenged to be the presence of God to others, including our children
Theme	Passing the Presence
Word	Mark 5:21-42
Metaphor/Image	Picture frames/ vintage-type decor
Synopsis	While honoring our fathers is a great place to start, this celebration is designed to speak to men in every stage of life. As parents or role models of any kind, we can only give out of what we have ourselves. On this special weekend we stress the need to, first of all, experience God's presence in our own lives, then to become impassioned to pass that Presence to those who look to us for their "picture of God."
Enhancement Ideas	Highlights in this celebration include a large altar table displaying vintage pictures, albums, christening gowns, and the like. Opening with "Teach Your Children Well," including the feature tune "Butterfly Kisses," and involving a small group of children singing during the song celebration are significant pieces of the occasion. Film clips and a closing prayer for men offered by six women put the final touches on a celebration that honors and challenges men of all ages.
Featured Options	Adult and children's choir together Heaven Is in My Heart

Worship Celebration

Opening Music

Band and Vocalists
Light band; project worship graphic; kids come up from front floor area

Teach Your Children Well
(by Crosby, Stills, and Nash)

Video Clip

From "Parenthood"
House lights down; begin immediately

Cowboy Dan at the birthday party

Call To Worship

Host
Light drama area; project graphic

It's scary how far we are willing to go sometimes in order to be whoever our kids need us to be at the time. Jesus even commented in the Gospel of Matthew that most of us wouldn't give our kids a stone if they asked us for bread. We want to do the right thing.

The good news is that we don't have to all be Cowboy Dan. Today we come to accept the challenge to be the presence of God for our families, to go beyond doing everything right to actually "Passing the Presence" on, right into our very own homes.

Listen now as the choir leads us in worship.

Song Celebration

Choir/Kids and male lead
Light choir and band

Heaven Is In My Heart

Band
Band leader asks congregation to stand/ project words

Rejoice
Always

Offering/Transition

Host
Light drama area; project

Everyone wants to feel like they're making a difference, yet some days the agenda is simply to hang on until bed time. The hope of making a difference gets put on the back burner . . . or at least we think it's on the back burner. Kids have a way of surprising us, though. The potential of our presence in their lives is often bigger than we think.

Video Clip

From "Parenthood"
House lights down

Goodnight scene in kid's bedroom

Featured Music

Band with male lead
Light band; with graphic enhancement

Butterfly Kisses
(by Bob Carlisle)

Message

Speaker
Light sermon area

"Passing the Presence"

Prayer For Men

Various Women; Host closes
Light platform; soft music under; maintain worship graphic

Father, we all want to do the right thing We want to allow your presence to come to life wherever we are. We come to you today to pray for men everywhere, for those who are here and those who are part of our lives each day.

Lord, we pray for men struggling with pain from past hurts, for those who haven't experienced the love of a father of their own. We ask you to make our Father's love real to them.

Jesus, so many we know have been directly affected by divorce, whether their own or their parents'. Be the strength these men need to become whole again. Mend the broken places in their lives.

Lord, we pray for men learning to be dads and stepdads. Give them the ability to love unconditionally when their own abilities fail them, to go beyond what they do and feel on their own and love with your strength.

Lord, we pray for men to know what it is to be a safe haven for others. We pray for single men to find their identity in you, to treat their sisters with godly respect, and to see all of us as people made for your enjoyment.

Sometimes men find it difficult to display healthy affection. Jesus, be their model. Touch hearts with the warmth of your Spirit. Set them free to express what is now trapped inside their hearts.

Father, we pray that you would give men young and old the courage to be real, to speak out on your behalf, and to be your presence to others. Amen.

Exit Music

Band and Vocalists
Light band; maintain worship graphic

Teach Your Children Well

Celebration Nineteen

Remember Who You Are

Felt Need	To have authenticity/identity in Christ
Desired Outcome	To see our own integrity issues and deal with them no matter what
Theme	Remember Who You Are/Integrity
Word	Genesis 28:15-19
Metaphor/Image	Military dog tags
Synopsis	Our identity serves as a point of reference for how we live our lives. This celebration message asserts that knowing who we are and *whose* we are is the key to living out our identity in God's truth.
Enhancement Ideas	Dog tags seem the perfect metaphor for illustrating who we are. Opening and closing music alludes to the enlightening experience of being sure of who we are—"I Can See Clearly Now."

Worship Celebration

Opening Music

Band

I Can See Clearly Now
(by Johnny Nash)

Light band; project candle graphic

Call To Worship

Host

Project worship graphic on cue (see script)

It's not always easy to remember who we are! We get deep into the everyday of life and lose sight of our main point of identification: Jesus. The awareness of his presence prompts us to refocus and remember who we are. His final words here on earth were words of reassurance he knew we would need to see things clearly. He said

"Remember, I am with you always" (Matthews 28:20, NRSV).

Let's stand now and celebrate his presence together.

Song Celebration

Band

Always
We Come To Praise You

Light band; project words; band leader seats after "We come . . ."

Host

Prayer

Let's pray together.

Father God, here in this place
  we seek your face,
    and Lord, we worship you.

Thank you for the privilege of all it means to be the people of God, the people of Jesus. We worship here together, aware of your presence. We are aware that you have promised to never leave us or abandon us. You come and remind us of *who* we are in you. You also assure us of *whose* we are and the deep connection we have to a loving Creator. In times of potential confusion, you become a still point, the presence we need so much to remind us of who we are.

We do give you all glory and honor and praise. We worship you.

Band

Song Celebration (continued)

Worship You

Continue with soft instrumental during prayer and segue into "Worship You"

Introduction to Video

Host
No graphic

Video
House lights down

Mission Moment

Host

Follow-Up/Announcements

Project announcements

Host

Offering

We give our time and resources to invest in ministry that reaches far beyond ourselves. Will the ushers come at this time to receive God's tithes and our offerings.

Band with male lead

Featured Music

Light band; project worship graphic

Here With Me
(by REO Speedwagon)

Speaker

Message

Light sermon area; 2 video clips from City Slickers

"Remember Who You Are"

Speaker

Closing Words

Project worship graphic

Band

Exit Music

Light band; worship graphic

I Can See Clearly Now

Celebration Twenty

Traveling Companions

Felt Need   To have companions on our journey with Christ

Desired Outcome   To include others in our journey; motivation toward small groups

Theme   Traveling Companions

Word   Acts 4:32-37

Metaphor/Image   "The Wizard of Oz" travelers

Synopsis   The journey of the Christian life was never meant to be attempted as a solo flight. Our need has always been to be connected to a group of people. We play out this theme through the metaphor of the four main "Wizard of Oz" characters. Drawing from the relationships between Dorothy, the Lion, the Scarecrow, and the Tin Man, we learn what it means to be people of promise to one another—advocates as Jesus is for us.

Enhancement Ideas   Aside from the expected video clips and great music this celebration contains, the highlight of the celebration is the Oz characters coming to life in a contemporary rendition of what it meant for the four of them to live in community. (Having just the right players is a must for this drama!) The large altar table presents a unique visual enhancement also. Yellow bricks ascending in height to create a "road" affect and candles placed on the road represent the light of Christ and community. Because nearly everyone is familiar with this movie, it provides a powerful way to connect people with their own need for traveling companions.

Worship Celebration

Opening Music

Band; jazz instrumental

Somewhere Over the Rainbow

Lights band; project instrumentalists

Opening Video Clip

From "The Wizard of Oz"

Lion joins the other Oz characters and the four become a team on the Yellow Brick Road.

House lights down; begin immediately after opening music

Call To Worship

Host

Maintain last frame of video clip as a graphic.

You and I are on a journey too. And even though we're human beings, we also frequently suffer from incompleteness. Empty hearts, fried brains, emotional homelessness; we know what these are like. We know where to go for help, but the journey is seldom easy and was never meant to be a solo act. The word for today: DO NOT ATTEMPT THIS ALONE.

We come to worship as a group, to do it a thousand times better than any of us could worship alone. Jesus said where several of us are gathered in his name, he is there in the middle. Let's stand to sing and enjoy his presence together.

Band

Light band; project words; host seats congregation

Song Celebration

Love Is What We've Come Here For
We Come To Praise You
Surely the Presence

Host

Soft music under; project worship graphic

Prayer

Prayer is talking to God, telling him the good, the bad, and the ugly. Today as we celebrate what it means to be the body of Christ it seems appropriate that we would take time to speak out for those among us with needs, and to stand on their behalf, taking on their concerns as our own. As we experience this time together, I encourage you to stand right where you are and say the name out loud of the person or family you are acquainted with that may have special needs. Remain standing and we will finish praying together.

pause for response

**Lord, There are burdens that we carry everyday;
sometimes they make us want to cry.
Hopeless feelings harbor deep inside our hearts,
and we find it hard to hold our heads up high.**

And then you send someone along to travel with us. Today we stand on behalf of others who have great needs, needs that you alone can know and address. We pray for healing, for grace, for strength in dark times. We pray for new light, new hope, fresh starts. Most of all today we pray that no one leave this place without knowing that you are here with them, alive and living in your people. You assure us that we need not attempt this journey alone.

We see you Lord. We worship you. Amen.

Traveling Companions

Song Reprise

Surely the Presence

Band
Light band; no words projected

Transition/Offering

Host
Project worship graphic

At the center of who we seek to be in this body of Christ is a real desire to carry out ministry that occurs within these walls and reaches out far beyond into the community and the world. Let's take time to help make that possible by giving out of our own resources as the ushers come to receive our offerings.

Featured Music

I'll Be There For You
(by The Rembrandts)

Band
Light band; project with worship graphic intermittently; drama players enter at end

Drama

Four players   "Friends"
House lights down; light drama area; project players

This is a sketch reminiscent of the characters in The Wizard Of Oz. *It is present day and these people are late teens/early twenties and have been in a small group together. They display characteristics that relate them to Oz characters; for example, Lyn paces when he walks and holds a cord in his hands that he plays with nervously (like the lion's tail). Scott's clothes have a ragged look, and he's always falling off his chair. Huck is tall and stiff, wearing a lot of silver jewelry; he has a Three-in-One can that he uses frequently to "oil" his elbows and knees. Dodie wears a modern blue-and-white-checked sun dress and red sandals; she has braids and carries a basket for a purse.*

Enter Huck (Tin Man), Lyn (Lion) and Scott (Scarecrow). They take their places on stage and assume a relaxed conversational position. LIGHTS UP

Huck   I should be studying.

Lyn   Wrong. You should be right here talking to us. It's the last time we have to get together before I start my summer job and then who knows when we'll see each other.

Scott   I just wish we could put this whole summer on pause. When Dodie goes away to school and I move to Illinois it's going to be tough to stay in touch. I've enjoyed traveling together.

Huck   Traveling?

Scott   Well, yeah. Traveling. Like we've been on a journey together. Sort of a yellow-brick-road type deal.

Others react with some confusion. Enter Dodie, excitedly waving a piece of mail.

Dodie   Hey! It came! I got accepted at Kansas State!

All share congrats and reluctant excitement

Dodie   Hey guys. This isn't the end of the world. We're going different directions for awhile, that's all. (*She pauses to reflect on some feelings.*) I just need to say that having this time to pray and talk with

124

you guys every week has been about the best thing that ever happened to me. You guys know how stupid I was when I first became a Christian. I thought being a Christian would mean no more problems. I always wanted to go and find a place where there wouldn't be any trouble. I really thought life could be like that—the Rainbow Syndrome. Needless to say, trouble's everywhere. You can't escape it. Boy did I find that out! Hey, it's not like I can really control anything, especially my relationships with the people I live with.

Huck   But you're doin' OK Dodie. Really OK. You've come a long, long way since I first met you and you've given me a lot too. *(shyly)* All of you have.

Scott   *(limply falls off chair and gets back up)* It's like, I never really knew what it meant to feel close to people. My own family, well, I've told you what a pain it was to be the youngest—and have the lowest average IQ on any given day. Good old brother Allan was the smart one. Allan had all the answers. The valedictorian; 4.0; full ride to Yale and back again; studly guy. Yep. He definitely had the brains in the family. *(sighs)* If I only had a brain.

Dodie   Don't say that Scott. You've helped me find answers to a lot of tough questions. You always have great insights for what I need at the time. *(She leans over to pick a piece of straw out from under his collar.)* What's this?

Scott   I don't know. Clueless. *(He falls off the chair again.)*

Lyn   It's amazing when I think back. I've told you guys stuff I would never open up about before. I've always hated talking about myself, especially my fears. My whole life has been pretty much fear-driven. Afraid to talk. Afraid to open up. Afraid to take risks. It never seemed like the right time. I'm basically a coward in recovery.

Huck   That's weird because when I first met you, you acted like you had it all together. You actually scared me.

Lyn   Yeah, well that was my mask. I'd had it on for about nineteen years. I think I was born with it on. But being around all of you has helped me see that it's OK to be real. It's like you and God make this big safety net around me that says "go ahead and be yourself. Step out with your faith. We'll be here no matter what."

Dodie   Yeah. And when I see you take those big steps of faith it reminds me to step out, too. *(looking over at Huck who is massaging a stiff elbow)* What's wrong with your arm? Did you hurt it again?

Huck   I think I'm just going to have to get used to this. The doctor says it's an inflammation in the joints. I can't stop moving or they get really stiff. He gave me a new drug to try out but it's supposed to be a chronic thing. Fun, huh?

Dodie   I wish it didn't have to be you.

Huck   Well why not me? I figure I have it pretty good. Other than my health, I feel great. When I think about it, just feeling at all is pretty great. I walked around numb for a long time before I found God and met up with you guys.

Lyn   And now?

Huck   Now—now I register emotion, *(sing-songy)* jealousy, devotion.

Dodie   OK!

Huck   What I'm trying to say is that . . . being part of your lives gives me this attached kind of feeling. Sorry. I don't mean to sound weird. It comes from my heart. *(He motions to his chest.)*

Scott   It's the Jesus Factor. *(He falls off his chair again.)*

Lyn   Get a grip, Scott.

Scott   Sorry.

Dodie   *(brushing dog hair off her clothing)* Dog hair. To-to-ly disgusting. All I know is that you're the best friends anybody ever had and it's funny, but I feel as though I've known you all my life. But I couldn't have, could I?

(All look at each other, shake their heads, and shrug.)

Dodie   *(continuing)* I'll miss you all. I feel like when we're here together, Jesus is here too. I've actually gotten to know God through all of you. You're like brothers to me. More than friends. Family. Right here in my own back yard. And as the old saying goes—

All   There's no place like home!

Blackout

Message

Speaker
Light sermon area

"Traveling Companions"

Closing Words

Host
Project worship graphic

Today you may have been challenged to find traveling companions or you may be unsure of how you can be there for someone else. Go now and be sons and daughters of encouragement as you travel in the presence of God. Amen.

Exit Music

Band
Light band and vocalists; continue with worship graphic

I'll Be There For You

*Consider an action step for small groups in your own setting.

Celebration Twenty-one

Why Jesus?

Felt Need   To identify totally with one Lord—Identity

Desired Outcome   To wholeheartedly claim the name of Jesus

Theme   Why Jesus?

Word   Acts 4:1-12

Metaphor/Image   Capstones

Synopsis   Being a seeker-sensitive congregation compels us to purposefully speak the message in a language people can understand, so from time to time we must backpedal and take time to explain a biblical metaphor. This weekend we rediscover the value of Jesus as the "capstone of our faith." The name of Jesus is the only name under heaven that requires a decision to be made on our part. Jesus is God's choice, the "capstone" of our faith. Just in case someone wouldn't know what a capstone is, this celebration explains the metaphor through a video produced in the spirit of Bill Nye the Science Guy, a Public Television children's show host.

Enhancement Ideas   A striking metaphor for the theme of "Why Jesus?" is that of a cornerstone or capstone. Without capstones, arches and whole buildings will fall. In order to teach this to a modern-day congregation, use a video. Teaching is also enhanced by a large charcoal drawing on an easel on the platform. "Why Jesus?"

Worship Celebration

Opening Music

Band   Jesus Is Just All Right With Me
Light band and vocalists; project   (by The Doobie Brothers)

Opening Video

"What Is a Capstone?"
House lights down; begin immediately after opening music; choir enters

Call To Worship

Host
Project capstone graphic and maintain; host asks congregation to stand

(Read Ephesians 2:19-22) "God is building a home. He's using you, fitting you in brick by brick, stone by stone with Jesus as the capstone that holds all the parts together."

What we really have to celebrate today is Jesus. God's absolute only choice to provide us the central source of life we so very much need. Let's stand to worship and celebrate this one who's name is above all other names: Jesus.

Song Celebration

Band and Choir   Lord I Lift Your Name On High
                                                                                     Glorify Thy Name
Light band and choir; project words; band leader seats congregation   We Believe In God

Prayer

Host
Continue with soft music under; project worship graphic only

So many unique people here today. So many different needs represented.

As you came through these doors today, you most likely had some sort of prayer on your heart. An issue that followed you here.

Our needs are different. Perhaps that is why Jesus is described with so many different names in the Old and New Testaments. Listen now as you consider which name speaks to your need today.

The Healer	Wonderful	The Light
The Great Physician	Counselor	The Door
Emmanuel, God With Us	Mighty God	The Living Water
Friend of Sinners	Everlasting Father	The Great I Am
Redeemer	Prince of Peace	

Whatever your need, wherever you've been, Jesus is here for you today. He desires to meet you where you are. Silently now, picture him as the one who comes to you.

Jesus, we all need you. Thank you for the extent of your ability to meet us where we are. To speak peace, to give counsel, to shed light in dark places. To be the door to God we so desperately need. To be Lord of All. We serve you because you are the Great I Am and have proven yourself over and over. We don't need great ideas, we need a mighty God on a daily basis. Thank you for who you are. Name above all names. We worship you Jesus. Amen.

Song Reprise

Band and Choir
Light band and choir; project words

We Believe In God

Why Jesus?

Host
Project worship graphic; choir exits

Announcements/Offering

Band with female lead
Light band; project

Featured Music

Say the Name
(by Margaret Becker)

Speaker
Light sermon area

Message

"Why Jesus?"

Band
Light band; project words

Closing Song

No Other Name

Speaker
Project speaker

Closing Words/Prayer

Band
Light band; maintain worship graphic

Exit Music

Jesus Is Just All Right With Me

Life-Givers: A Communion Celebration

Felt Need	Possibilization—To know I have potential to affect the lives of others
Desired Outcome	To realize and use our ability to spark life in others
Theme	Life-Givers
Word	Exodus 20:13; Matthew 5:21-22; John 4:1-30
Metaphor/Image	Wishing wells and water containers
Synopsis	What a powerful concept that, as children of God, we have the ability to be life-givers to others. Simple life-giving acts can change the world one person at a time. This celebration is ripe with potential to help us realize our own abilities to know the true Life-Giver and to pass that Life onto others everyday.
Enhancement Ideas	Using the story of the woman Jesus encountered at the well (John 4), the natural metaphor for this celebration is the picture of a well. The opening music, Eric Clapton's "Change the World," sparks great feeling for the theme and sets up the congregation to want to know more. Later, through the dramatic storytelling and sermon, the message is driven home. Communion can then become a tangible experience of passing the Life to others.
Featured Option	Communion Celebration

Worship Celebration

Opening Music

Change the World
(by Eric Clapton)

Male lead and guitar
Light vocalist; project appropriate graphic

Call To Worship
"If You Could Change Your World . . ."

Host
Project worship graphic; host invites congregation to stand

If you could change someone's world, how would you do it? If you had one day to walk into someone's life and do something that would last forever, what would your plan be?

Jesus had a plan to change the world and he came to share it with those who chose to accept the challenge. It was a simple plan. Take his life, the living water we need so much, and give it to others, one person at a time, through simple life-giving acts. Become life-givers from the inside out.

Let's join together now to celebrate Jesus, our Life-Giver.

Song Celebration

Rejoice
Turn Your Eyes Upon Jesus
(UMH, # 349)
Shine On Us

Band
Light band; project words; band leader seats us

Prayer

Host

Continue with light music under; worship graphic only; project prayer

Will you pray with me now?

Thank you, Lord, for shining on all of us in so many ways. We have seen your hand of grace. We have been the recipients of many life-giving acts, and we want to thank you.

Father, we live in a difficult place. Out of our desire to get ahead or control our individual desires to get ahead or to control our circumstances we often become life-takers. We confess that our words and actions have taken their toll. At times we have snuffed the very life out of those we live and work with.

Lord God, forgive us. Many times we haven't known what we were doing. Change our hearts as the light of your love shines on us today. We worship you as the one who comes to bring us health and healing. In the name of Jesus, Amen.

Song Reprise

Band

Light band; project words

Shine On Us

Video/Offering

Host

Project worship graphic

Featured Music

Band

Light band; project worship graphic

Only Here for a Little While
(by Billy Dean,
from "Greatest Hits")

Storytelling

Adult female

"He Changed Her World"

Light drama area after player enters; project; house lights down

She hadn't really planned to see anyone that day at the well. Experience had taught her when to go for water so that she could safely come and go to avoid the painful glares of disdain.

His plan was to catch a few winks while the boys went to town for food. And what better place to rest than a well at noon? No one comes for water at this hour. So he sat down, stretched his arms, and leaned against the wall of the well. But his nap was soon interrupted. He opened one eye just enough to see her trudging up the trail with a heavy jar on her shoulder. Behind her came half a dozen kids, each one looking like a different daddy.

She didn't really have to say a word. Her life story was written on the wrinkles of her face. The wounds of five broken romances were gaping and festered. Each man who had left her had taken a piece of her heart. Life-takers. Now she wasn't sure there was anything left.

"And the man you now live with won't even give you his name." Jesus said it for her. He understood her pain too well. Far more than five men had broken commitments to him.

Silently the Life-Giver reached into his kit and pulled out a needle of faith and a thread of hope. In the shade of Jacob's well he stitched her broken spirit back together. Words of life became her medicine as he spoke. "There will come a day when what you're called will not matter. The Father is out looking for those who are simply and honestly themselves before him."

No one would have blamed Jesus for ignoring the woman at the well that day. To have turned his head would have been much easier, less controversial, and not nearly as risky. But God, who made her, couldn't do that. God's a Life-Giver.

Message

Speaker

"Life-Givers"

Light sermon area

Communion

Pastor-led
Band   Shine On Us

Light altar/light band 50 percent/maintain service graphic throughout; no word projection

Closing Words

Speaker
Project speaker

Exit Music

Band   Only Here for a Little While
Light band; project worship graphic

Coming Out of the Closet

Felt Need	To claim our own identity
Desired Outcome	To decide to unashamedly identify with Jesus
Theme	Out of the Closet
Word	Acts 4:13
Metaphor/Image	Doors, closets
Synopsis	While the phrase "coming out of the closet" is generally used in connection with the gay community, we were eager to express the need for us, as Christians, to come out of our closets of timidity and to boldly proclaim our faith, whatever the cost. However, it is always risky and costly to take a stand and be faithful. This celebration encourages us to quit kidding ourselves and begin to unashamedly identify with Jesus.
Enhancement Ideas	A lot of great, meaningful music combines well with drama that describes people's innate reluctance to take a stand. The "Reasonably Live" video gives the opportunity to create a video that looks live and interactive (as on the "Late Show") but was preproduced. This celebration feels "edgy" from beginning to end, a great time to contemplate "coming out of the closet."

Worship Celebration

Opening Music

Choir   One Less Stone
Light choir and band; project

Opening Segment/Introduce Video

Three players (including Host)   "Reasonably Live"

Begin with different choir or band members with microphones asking where the host is. Person X stands to say "I'll go get her" and then exits backstage. As that person walks through the hallway, we hear, from "backstage," the following conversation:

Person X   (Host?) (Host?) (Host!) *(Use his/her name.)*

Person B   I saw her go into that closet.

Person X   What? What in the . . . *(sound of opening door)*

Host   Hey!

Person X   Oh my gosh *(name)*. What in the world? What are you doing in the closet? We're all ready to have heart failure out there. We're waiting on you!

Host   I'm not coming out.

Person X   Huh?

Host   Find somebody else. Call the other worship leader. I'm not coming out.

Person X   Host, Be reasonable. This is your job. Actually it goes way beyond that. Oh whatever! Could you just pull it together and get this show on the road?

Host	No.
Person X	OK. Why?
Host	I just saw an old friend of mine right in the second row.
Person X	And that's a good thing, right?
Host	No. That's a bad thing.
Person X	OK, a bad thing. Why?
Host	She doesn't know me like this. She doesn't know me as the worship host.
Person X	And that's a bad thing, right?
Host	No, that's a good thing. If she saw that I was worship host, she'd think I was a, a, a fake. She doesn't know I'm a Christian.
Person X	And is that a bad thing or a good thing?
Host	Bad. I mean good. I mean, she'd flip out! I wasn't ever a Christian around her.
Person X	You, you mean you hid it from her.
Host	Well, let's just say I never got around to sharing that aspect of my life with her.
Person X	Well, now isn't that just great. And so we're down one worship leader, and I suppose I'm supposed to go out and tell everyone. My advice is to come out and face the music. Pull it together, girl.
Host	And what if I don't?

(The sound of a door being closed is heard; Person X returns to the stage and addresses the camera with fake composure.)

Person X	I'm sorry but we are temporarily experiencing technical difficulties. Please be patient and proceed with the worship celebration.

Featured Music

Band

House lights back up; light band and vocalists only (not choir); project worship graphic

I'm Coming Out
(by Diana Ross)

Call To Worship

Host

Project worship graphic

So, now that you've discovered where I hide out, let me ask you a question. Where's your closet? Where is it that you go into hiding? Where do you relinquish the radical identity of Jesus to be simply known as "that nice church person?"

Jesus spoke out from mountaintops; he did not mutter in valleys. He spoke in synagogues, streets, temples, gardens, and at every party he ever attended. He was not afraid to stand out in a crowd. In fact, he was totally unsuccessful at hiding who he was.*

We come today to experience the passionate call of Jesus and to respond boldly as he invites us to come out of the closet. Let's worship now.

Song Celebration

Band and Choir

Light choir and band; project words

Almighty God
I Wanna Be In the Light

Coming Out of the Closet

Prayer

Host
Soft music and choir begin transition to next song; project worship graphic

Dear God, we make a lot of dramatic statements about giving you our all, our whole lives. We proclaim you to be at the center of our lives, but our own actions often betray us. We have mixed passions, confused values.

Fire Of God, burn away what is not holy. Renew the passion of our first love. Hear the prayer of our hearts as we sing.

Song Celebration (continued)

Band and Choir   Fire Of God
Light band and choir; project words

Introduce Mission Moment

Host
Project host; choir exits

Mission Moment

Video
Lower house lights

Host
No projection

Follow-Up/Offering

Band
Light band; project special graphic; with brief speaking portion

Featured Music

Carry Me High
(by Rebecca St. James)

Speaker
Light sermon area

Message

"Out of the Closet"

Speaker

Prayer/Send Out

Band
Light band; project worship graphic

Exit Music

I'm Coming Out

*Laurie Beth Jones, *Jesus, CEO* (New York: Hyperion, 1996), p. 116.

Who Are You?
A Welcome Weekend Celebration

Felt Need   Identity

Desired Outcome   We would know who we are in Christ

Theme   Identity

Word   Psalms 100:3

Metaphor/Image   Fingerprints

Synopsis   Although we are continuously searching out and
                         speaking to pre-Christians, several times a year we
                         design events that are even more intentionally
                         designed to reach people who have little or no
                         church background. This particular celebration was
                         a part of our fall "Welcome Weekend" and
                         addresses our universal felt need of identity: to
                         understand who God is and, in turn, who we are.

Enhancement Ideas   Something we all possess is our unique fingerprint. Fin-
                         gerprints are totally unique and become a simple, nat-
                         ural way of establishing identity. Playing on this
                         metaphor, use the prayer time to talk to people about
                         how amazing their own fingerprints are. Featuring
                         great music and a winning Top Ten List, this celebration
                         builds a bridge between God's heart and our guests.

Worship Celebration

Opening Music

Band
Light band; project fingerprint graphic

Who Are You?
(by The Who)

Call To Worship

Host
House lights down; light Host at center stage.

Who are you? It's easy to become downright confused about who you are. In fact, maybe you started out confused and never fully recovered.

Or maybe you thought you knew who you were, but there were others who sharply disagreed and *they* began to determine your identity.

So it's easy to forget who we are or to never really know in the first place. We've come here today to be reminded of who we are and whose we are. To come face to face with the amazing God who gives to each of us a unique identity. Let's stand to sing and worship together.

Song Celebration

Band and Choir
Choir comes up at beginning; light band and choir when choir in place; project words

Amazing Grace

Choir/female lead
Segue into choir; continue lighting ; project choir and lead

I Am Blessed

144

Prayer/Song

Host   Come Just As You Are

Light center stage; project fingerprint graphic; begin soft music when host reads scripture; begin vocal lead as host says "Amen"; project words as lead finishes

Tiny lines of flesh lace their way across the skin of your fingertips in distinctive patterns. They will never change, no matter how long you live. Each of your ten fingers is different. Even if the tips of your fingers are burned, the ridges will grow back in the same pattern you were born with. As you probably know, no two people have precisely the same prints.

So what does that mean? It means that no matter how you feel about yourself, God the Creator looks at you as unique and valuable. Whatever you may have done isn't nearly as important as who made you and whose you are. Look again at your fingerprint as I say a prayer from Psalm 139:

> Oh yes, you shaped me first inside, then out;
>   you formed me in my mother's womb.
> I thank you, High God—you're breathtaking!
>   Body and soul, I am marvelously made!
>   I worship in adoration—what a creation!
> You know me inside and out,
>   you know every bone in my body;
> You know exactly how I was made, bit by bit,
>   how I was sculpted from nothing into something.
> Like an open book, you watched me grow from conception to birth;
>   all the stages of my life were spread out before you,
> The days of my life all prepared
>   before I'd even lived one day (Psalm 139, *The Message*).

Thank you, God, for calling us to yourself just as we are, for you have made us just as we are. We are thankful that you would care for us and love us, and give us life. Amen.

Announcements

Host
Light center stage; choir exits

Top Ten List

Host 2
Continue lighting ; Host 2 interrupts Host 1; with sound effects from band and graphics

Top Ten Ways to Know You're in a Bad Church

10. The church bus has gun racks.

9. When dropping your kids off in the nursery, they ask for a damage deposit.

8. ATM in the lobby

7. Favorite hymn ends with "And Bingo was his name-o"

6. Services are B.Y.O.S.: "Bring Your Own Snake"

5. Choir wearing leather robes

4. No cover charge, but communion is a two drink minimum

3. Karaoke worship time

2. Ushers ask "Smoking or non-smoking?"

1. Good news: bottomless cups of coffee;
   Bad news: pay toilets

Offering

Host
Continue lighting; project worship graphic

Who Are You? A Welcome Weekend Celebration

Featured Music

Band

Lights on band; project

Spirit In the Sky
(From "Michael" soundtrack)

Message

Speaker

Light sermon area; Use video clip "What Is God Like?" close to the beginning

"Who Are You?"

Closing Words

Host

Light drama area; project beach graphic; band comes up from stage right

Exit Music

Band

Begin immediately when host finishes; light band; project worship graphic

Spirit In the Sky

Closing the Goodness Gap

Felt Need	Authenticity
Desired Outcome	To understand God's attempt to bridge the gap
Theme	Goodness Gap
Word	Psalms 51:1
Metaphor/Image	Large cavern with "good" as distant mountain shape

Synopsis

Sometimes we create our own insanity by trying so hard to be what we can never be: good. We want to do all the right things but end up feeling phony and fake. God alone is good, and when we figure that out and surrender control to the One who only is good, we then find our true, authentic selves. This celebration becomes a way to rediscover what Christ has done to close our Goodness Gap.

Enhancement Ideas

This celebration sets up well with the familiar Diana Ross tune "Ain't No Mountain High Enough." An appropriate follow-up is a video clip from Monty Python's "Holy Grail" depicting several characters humorously attempting to cross a giant divide. The produced video asks various people on the street what they think makes someone good. It is great to hear opinions from outside the church walls.

Worship Celebration

Opening Music

Band and Choir
House lights down; light band and choir; project service graphic

Ain't No Mountain
(by Diana Ross)

Video Clip

From "Monty Python and the Holy Grail"
Continue house lights down

The crusaders arrive at a bridge crossing.
An old man challenges them
with three questions.

Call To Worship

Host
Project worship graphic

"The Goodness Gap"

So often there is this really big gap between where we are in our lives and where we want to be. We teeter precariously at the edge of the gap, trying hard to maintain our image. We see the other side but we don't know how to get there on our own. Phoniness lurks in the gap.

We come to worship today to get honest about our own lack of goodness and to be challenged to close the gap.

Let's stand together as we anticipate what God will do.

Song Celebration

Band and Choir
Light band and choir; project words

Stand and See

Prayer

Host
Project prayer graphic; soft music under

Good worship helps us meet with God, face to face. It's not just about hearing what I *should* be like, but the opportunity to be honest about who I really am, in the face of a God who won't quit loving us no matter what. We know that there are inconsistencies in our lives, in our hearts *(hold up box)*, but so often we don't dare to open the lid *(open lid)* and look in for fear of being discovered. We use up a lot of our energy just trying to maintain our image, keep the lid on *(close lid)*.

Listen to these words of freedom from Psalm 139:

> Search me, O God, and know my heart;
>> test me and know my anxious thoughts.
> See if there is any offensive way in me,
>> and lead me in the way everlasting (vv. 23-24 NIV).

We all need a place of honesty. Take a moment of silence to lift the lid off of your secret heart and identify one inconsistency you are aware of. Take some time to confess to God one place where you know *you* can't, but *God* can.

Pause for reflection

Lord, God, search us and know us. We're not where we want to be. Guide us on the road to life, real life in you. Amen.

Song Celebration (continued)

Band
Light band; project words

Create In Me A Clean Heart
Lord, You Are More Precious

Closing the Goodness Gap

Host
Project mission graphic; choir exits

Announcements

Band with male lead
Light band; continue with prayer graphic

Featured Music

Heart of Gold
(by Neil Young)

"What Is a Good Person?"
House lights down; no formal introduction

Video

Speaker
Light sermon area

Message

"Closing the Goodness Gap"

Host
Project prayer graphic

Closing Words

You were wired for goodness so don't hide out. *(Open box)* Get honest with God and trust him to close the goodness gap. Amen.

Band
Light band; project worship graphic

Exit Music

Ain't No Mountain

Celebration Twenty-six

Honest to God

Felt Need

To be totally honest and authentic

Desired Outcome

To experience a time of confession and leave with a fresh beginning for life

Theme

Honest to God

Word

2 Samuel 11:27

Metaphor/Image

Coral reef—going below the surface

Synopsis

Honesty with God is a tough place to go for a lot of people. Realizing that many of us tend to show others our "surface selves," we wanted to communicate getting past the surface of our lives so that we may deal with whatever lurks below. Great visuals, humorous drama, and a time for confession serve to make this celebration a straight shot. Notice also a real diversion from our more "normal" structure. Such a change can be refreshing and serve to strengthen the message.

Enhancement Ideas

For this message we placed a large fish tank on the altar table. Floating candles are on the surface of the water; however, various debris lurks below: an old leather shoe, a 45 record, some "junk," and a few goldfish for interest. During the Call To Worship the host might lean forward and swish the water. The drama is a refreshing reminder of how we even lie to ourselves (but beware, it requires a great Jim Carrey clone). This is a great celebration and a deep challenge to get honest with God in our lives.

Worship Celebration

Song Celebration

Band

Light platform when band is in place; project words

Lord I Lift Your Name on High
Heaven Is In My Heart
I Waited for the Lord

Video Clip

Underwater Life

Science documentary footage that shows
the marvels found below the ocean surface

House lights down; begin immediately following music

Call To Worship/Prayer

Host

"Below the Surface"

Project worship graphic; begin soft music under prayer; project prayer response at end of prayer followed by song words

A body of water is such an amazing phenomenon. Above the surface, a beautiful glistening reflection of light and shadow, a display of ongoing serenity. Break below the surface, however, and encounter a totally different world. Fish, rocks, plants, and debris inhabit this environment, totally oblivious to the world above.

Our lives are like that. There's the surface aspect that everyone sees, but break below the surface and we encounter a totally different space. It's amazing to think about what lurks down there. Many times it's a hidden world of its own. Today we come to learn that real life can only happen as we plunge below the surface of our lives, as we become totally honest with the One who is truth: Jesus.

Prayer

Host
Continuing on after Call to Worship without a break

As we join together for prayer, let's first take a moment to say out loud the stuff of life that we are thankful for today. Feel free to speak out right where you are and say a word of thanks to God.

Pause for response

Begin soft music.

Thank you God. Next, let's take time to go a bit further below the surface. Sometimes we come to worship hoping for a fresh start but we really must do the hard work of confession, of being clear in our hearts about wrongs done to others, impatience, hurtful language, and selfish attitudes. Take a few moments now to silently confess what actions you have done, intentionally or unintentionally, to separate you from God and others.

Pause for silent prayer

Going below the surface isn't always comfortable, but while we have our heads bowed, dare with me to go deeper still. Tell God what he already knows about the deepest part of you. Not so much what you may have *done* wrong, but anything that may lurk at the bottom: unresolved issues that plague you and you've not felt safe enough to disclose to anyone. In the safety of this room, be willing to silently be open and vulnerable before a loving and personal God.

Pause for silent prayer

As we end this time of prayer, will you say with me the words from Psalm 51 that now appear on the screen?

Create in me a clean heart, O God, and put a new and right spirit within me.

Restore to me the joy of your salvation, and sustain in me a willing spirit. Amen (vv. 51:10, 12).

Honest to God

Song Celebration Continued

Band
Light band; project words when vocals start

Come Just as You Are
Oh Lord, You're Beautiful

Announcements

Host
Graphic enhancement; Host calls for ushers

Offering/Featured Music

Band
Light band; project worship graphic

Honesty
(by Billy Joel)

Drama

Two players: one older female therapist and.   "Liar Liar"
one "Jim Carrey"-type male

House lights down; light drama area; buzzer and voice from above; project players

"Liar Liar"

Lights up on Dr. T. standing in drama area; buzzer sounds immediately

Dr. T.   *(leaning down to answer intercom)* Yes?

Receptionist   Your three o'clock is here, Dr. Truth.

(voice only)

Dr. T.   Send him in.

Receptionist   I'd love to. He's a regular pain in the you-know-what.

Fletcher runs in and slides onto drama area and into Dr. T.'s face

Fletcher   How was your weekend?

Dr. T.   Did you . . . have any trouble getting in?

Fletcher   No more than usual, thank you. Your receptionist is a real gem.

Dr.   I see. Make yourself comfortable please.

Fletcher goes through assorted gyrations on the couch.

Dr. T.   So, Mr. Deed. You're here because you have an ongoing and increasingly annoying addiction to lying. As we've discussed, honesty comes hard for you. Lately we've been talking about new and better ways of dealing with reality. How are things going this week?

Fletcher   Well it depends on how far back you want to go.

Dr. T.   Let's talk about this morning.

Fletcher	This morning? I can't talk about today. I'm still too worried about yesterday. And the day before. And the week before. And last year. *(Fletcher falls off the couch)*
Dr. T.	Are you all right?
Fletcher	I'll thank you not to ask such personal questions.
Dr. T.	It sounds like you're still experiencing some anxiety, no doubt resulting from attempting to cover up what's on the inside.
Fletcher	Ding ding ding! What do we have for her, Johnny?
Dr. T.	Mr. Deed, you're a very sick man.
Fletcher	Good call. *(lying down, then getting back up)* But illness can mean so many things.
Dr. T.	Could we get to the point?
Fletcher	*(standing and singing)* Here she comes to wreck the day!
Dr. T	Fletcher!
Fletcher	Yes mother?
Dr. T.	Fletcher, calm down. You can never really get any better until you begin to deal with why you lie. You lie to avoid painful issues and who you are deep down. You lie because you're out of the habit of telling the truth. You've got to come clean. Remember, you're not the first person on the planet to have to deal with these issues.
Fletcher	I'm getting what I deserve. I'm reaping what I sow. I . . . *(clasps hands over mouth)*
Dr. T.	Mr. Deed, you can beat this. Dare to go below the surface. You may find some beautiful specimens underneath all that . . . pond scum.
Fletcher	That's a nice image—deleted!
Dr. T.	You're doing it again.
Fletcher	What?

Dr. T.   Continuing to make light of what is so very important. Fletcher, it's OK to not be perfect. It's OK to not be everyone's favorite human being. It's OK to not have everything together. You have to learn to accept yourself. You've got to practice being honest.

Fletcher   *(standing up to leave)* OK, OK . . . *(thinking)* Dr. Truth, do you think I'll ever get well?

Dr. T.   *(Flustered, groping for words, Dr. T. stands and obviously crosses her fingers behind her back.)* Well, uh, yes! It's just a matter of time!

Blackout

Speaker
Light sermon area

Message

"Honest to God"

Host
Project worship graphic; band on stage with Host; Host bends down to swish her hand into the aquarium

Closing Words

Don't settle for a surface relationship with God. Break below the surface and get real. Walk in honesty this week. Amen.

Band
Light band; project worship graphic

Exit Music

I Waited for the Lord

Celebration Twenty-seven

Give It Up:
A Communion Celebration

Felt Need	Security
Desired Outcome	To discover the source of security who will provide us with risk-taking faith
Theme	Give It Up
Word	Psalm 121
Metaphor/Image	Security blankets
Synopsis	Just as most of us shared the childhood need of a security blanket, as adults we all cling to something that we perceive allows us security and safety. Clinging to a person, experience, or addiction keeps us from experiencing true faith rooted in the security God gives. To possess risk-taking faith, we must give up the blankets and cling to God alone. What a great metaphor for all that holds us back!
Enhancement Ideas	A plethora of authentic baby and security blankets adorn the altar table along with candles and the communion elements. The clip from Mr. Mom sets up the celebration very well. The choir piece "You Were There" comes very highly recommended with a strong lead. Communion then provides a tangible experience that enhances a simple but very effective celebration.
Featured Option	Communion

Worship Celebration

Song Celebration

Band and Choir

Light band and choir; project words for "Where Do I Go?"

Where Do I Go?
Jesus Is Just All Right

Video Clip

From "Mr. Mom"

House lights down; begin immediately

Giving up the "wooby"

Call To Worship

Host

Project worship graphic

"Blankets We Hold On To"

The security blanket. It's good for so many things. It's amazing how one piece of cloth can be a warm cover, a pillow, a cape, a Kleenex, a tablecloth, a washcloth, a friend. Chances are most of us here had a security blanket of some sort. Kids need 'em, sure, but truth is adults never really outgrow our need for security. We just find more sophisticated blankets.

The radical call of Jesus to us today is to shed the blankets, to give up our home-grown sources of security, and to go forward with the only One who can truly be trusted.

Puts the blanket down on the altar and continues on

Prayer With Response

Host continues
Project responsive prayer; lower house lights

It really is about trust; not just belief, but childlike trust. Together in prayer we can remind ourselves to trust God by restating the faithfulness God has displayed to us so many times in the past. In Psalm 124, David sings of Israel's deliverance, asking the question, "What if?"

Together now, let's join in speaking the words from this Psalm as a prayer of praise for deliverance in our lives with the words "If the Lord had not been on our side . . ."

Let's pray together:

Congregation	***If the Lord had not been on our side . . .***
Host	We would not have been able to stay clear of evil yesterday.
Congregation	***If the Lord had not been on our side . . .***
Host	The anger and rage of others would have consumed us this morning.
Congregation	***If the Lord had not been on our side . . .***
Host	We would have lost sight of a steady, clear course for tomorrow.
Congregation	***If the Lord had not been on our side . . .***
Host:	We would be alone. Oh blessed God; Who did not go off and leave us, our help is in the name of the Lord who made heaven and earth. *(Psalm 124, author's paraphrase)*

Possibly you have had an experience of your own that enabled you to see beyond all doubt that God is real and trustworthy. It had to be God. Sharing that experience out loud can actually become a public declaration of God's goodness whereby we encourage one another. The microphones are set up for you. In a brief statement, finish this sentence. "It had to be God when . . ."

While you're thinking about it, I'll go first. "It had to be God when_____ *(Host finishes, modeling brevity)*

Prayers of the People

Host closes when appropriate; allow for people to speak from microphones; begin playing "I Love You Lord" softly; project worship graphic; begin softly playing next song when Host closes

Let's pray together now in closing.

Eternal God, we see your hand. We know your heart. Help us, Lord, to learn to trust. Help us not just to believe on the sidelines, but to trust you right in the middle of life. Thank you for showing yourself to be faithful and true. We love you Lord. Amen.

Prayer in Song

Band   I Love You Lord
Light band and choir; project words   We Believe In God

Announcements

Host
Project graphic support

Offering/ Featured Music

Choir with female lead   You Were There
Light choir and band; project; choir and band exit following   (by Brooklyn Tabernacle Choir)

Message

Speaker   "Give It Up"
Light sermon area

162

Give It Up: A Communion Celebration

Communion

Pastor-led
Light altar; altar shot as graphic; band plays instrumental music

Closing Words

Host
Project worship graphic

The radical call of Jesus is to give up the private altars, the security blankets. Stand sure in the shadow of the One you can trust. Amen.

Worship: The Big Picture

Felt Need	To see new possibilities for our lives
Desired Outcome	To begin to see all of life from God's perspective
Theme	The Big Picture
Word	Psalm 122:1-9
Metaphor/Image	Picture frames
Synopsis	We are fervent about communicating worship as a lifestyle rather than a weekly ritual. This celebration describes worship as going beyond the religious exercise to actually seeing God, to live our lives in view of the Big Picture. We identify the metaphor of picture frames. This celebration is a part of our annual season of stewardship. We begin with God's perspective, an attitude of worship.
Enhancement Ideas	Gather a large variety of picture frames of various colors and sizes including one especially large frame to serve as a centerpiece. Hang these frames in different places throughout the sanctuary. The "Thoughts From the Stools" piece is a great example of a type of Reader's Theater, another way to tell a story that fosters a conversational spirit with the congregation.

Worship Celebration

Opening Music

Worship You

Band (instrumental)
Light band only; no projection

Music (continued)

Female lead (a cappella)
Dim lights on band; lights up on center stage; no projection once through chorus

Song Celebration

Worship You

Band
Light band; project words

Call To Worship

Host   "The Big Picture"

House lights down; maintain graphic

The Big Picture. We need to take a second look; to think about it. Just because some-one has witnessed a thousand rainbows doesn't mean that he's seen the magnificence of one. You can live near a garden and fail to focus on the beauty of a flower. And a person can be all that goodness calls her to be and still never see the Author of life.

Being moral or religious doesn't mean we will see God. We may see what others see in God, or hear what some say God said. But until we take a hard look at Jesus for ourselves and see life from God's perspective, the Big Picture will simply be a hazy form.

Today we come to be eyewitnesses of the God who calls us, and to be challenged to live our lives in view of the Big Picture. Stand with me now as we worship together.

Song Celebration

Band   We Come to Praise You

Light band; project words; band leader invites congregation to stand and be seated   Sing a Joyful Song

Thoughts From the Stools

Three speakers
Lights up on drama area; reduce house lights; project speakers

Three speakers are seated on tall stools in drama area, dialoging both with each other and to the audience, talk-show style. The letters they read are unique to Ginghamsburg Church and are included here as models to be replaced with stories from your own congregational setting.

Female   We come to worship each week and brush shoulders with hundreds of people but know very little about the experience of others.

Male 1   That's true. We get together and assume everyone comes from a similar vantage point, but in reality there are a lot of unique stories about what God is actually doing in different people's lives.

Male 2   We want to share some excerpts from feedback that we've received to help everyone get a better view of the Big Picture.

Male 1   One family explained, "We were invited by a coworker to come to worship but had to develop courage to visit, since church was not of any real interest to us. We had a great visit and were impressed with the attempt to reach out to us and others."

Female   A woman called a friend here and said that neither she nor her parents had ever known about church while growing up. She recently moved into this area and brought her parents to our church. Her father now calls her every Wednesday and wants to make sure they are planning to go to church on Sunday. He doesn't want to miss a week. The woman said her dad has opened his heart to Jesus, and the whole family is excited.

Male 2   One young mother was very honest about her experience. "In 1994 I ran into a girl from my high school who invited me to this church. I fell in love with the place on that day. I love everything here, from the nursery to the music, all the things that are done to help people, and the forthright style of ministering. I am amazed at how genuine people are. Almost every week that I have been here, I have felt like crying. Several people have told me that it's the Spirit working in me. It must be, because I hadn't cried in what seemed like years."

Male 1   One man shared his experience with this note: I have taken small steps toward becoming a better Christian since I have had the privilege of listening to the sermons. I have made the commitment to attend regularly, and I actually sing softly during the service now, something that previously was unheard of. I have attended some functions on Wednesday night and have volunteered to be an usher/greeter. I am doing this gradually and in small incremental steps since I'm not real comfortable with 'jumping in with both feet.' I am amazed at how quickly we felt comfortable, and we are anxious to become more involved. My only regret is that I wasted a lot of years when I could have been benefitting from this experience."

Male 2   This last note is really amazing. This man explains: "I am 51 years old and have never really believed in a deity. I'm an agnostic. I have visited your church for services for the past four consecutive weeks. I have never been so impressed with a church and the feeling of goodwill I experience among everyone present. I do have a question. Is it all right for me to keep coming even if I do not feel any sense of confidence that my belief system can be altered? Am I being hypocritical?"

Female   Wow. Honesty. We never know how worship affects others. Right now, we want to take some time to pray together. Would you all join us as we share our hearts with the Lord?

Guided Prayer

Speakers continue
Continue lighting; project worship graphic on screen; soft music under

Female   *(Bowing together)* Lord, we know many people here have needs that we can't possibly know about, but we do care. We want to pray silently for others around us right now and any concerns they may have brought with them tonight/today.

Pause for prayer

Male 1   Lord, as we hear these messages of hope that others have shared, I know that there are those I work with, those I see each day that need you. They need to see hope and life. We take time now to pray for them.

Pause for prayer

Male 2   And Lord, you put us in families and relationships with people to help shape and mold us. We pray now for those we hold closest to us, for the people we know best. We place them in your presence right now.

Pause for prayer

Female   Thank you, Lord, for hearing us tonight/today. We know that because of your love and care we can be sure you have heard us. In the name of Jesus, Amen.

Let's continue to worship now as the ushers come to receive the offerings we've brought to share.

Offering/Featured Music

Band with female lead   Love Has a Hold On Me
Light band; project with graphic intermittently   (by Amy Grant)

Message

Speaker   "Worship: The Big Picture"
Light sermon area

Song Of Response

Band   I Want To Be Where You Are
Light band; project words

Closing Words

Host
Project worship graphic

If I attempt to live life from my own limited perspective, I'll end up with an equally small life. Don't settle for anything less than the sight of the Big Picture every single day. It's a celebration! Amen!

Exit Music

Band
Light band; maintain worship graphic

Celebration
(by Kool and the Gang)

Blessed Are the Harnessed

Felt Need   To find freedom, inside and out

Desired Outcome   To serve through total submission to God

Theme   Authority: Blessed Are the Harnessed

Word   Psalm 123:1-2

Metaphor/Image   Yokes/harnesses

Synopsis   From time to time we address authority issues in the celebration messages as a clear understanding that God's authority is central to our own effectiveness in the Kingdom. "Blessed are the meek" may be better translated as "blessed are the harnessed." In this celebration we set up the theme with our own lighthearted video telling what it means to be harnessed and later a storytelling of the centurion soldier's experience regarding authority issues.

Enhancement Ideas   This is a great weekend for visual display. Several horse harnesses can be hung together on the platform. On the altar table place a huge authentic cattle yoke, another type of harness. This celebration winds up being the kind of experience that causes one to say, "Oh, I get it now!"

Worship Celebration

Opening Music

Band (instrumental)   Awesome God
Light band; project

Opening Video

"Yoked"
House lights down; begin immediately following band

Call To Worship

Host
House lights up; project worship graphic

When I walk our dog I can't help thinking "man, I am soooo glad I'm me not him! Nobody's got this girl on a leash. I'm thankful to be free to walk where I please, without anyone's jerking my chain."

Truth is none of us is as free as we think we are. We spend out lives trying to be free and inevitably wind up enslaved to something. The question is: Who's harness are we in? Who's holding the leash?

The issue today is authority. We come to be challenged to get into God's harness, to find out what Jesus meant when he said to "Take my yoke upon you"—because that's how we were created to live! We come to get into alignment with an awesome God, a holy God. Listen now as we begin our worship together.

Song Celebration

Band
Light band; project words

Holy, Holy, Holy
Blessed Be the Name
I Love You Lord

Prayer

Host leads with group participation
Project worship graphic; floor microphones for response; soft music at closing

"Let go and let God" is one of those catchy phrases we throw around once in a while, but stop and think how powerful it is. Let go and let God. Who among us hasn't had a time when we had some problem, some issue, that we simply couldn't handle. "I'm at the end of my rope. I just can't see my way out. I'm done." And you knew you had to let go and let God.

One reason we come together each week is to encourage one another with words of God's goodness and power. As you recall your own experience of letting go, we will all be encouraged as you share that experience out loud. The microphones are in place on the floor and in the balcony you can just stand to speak, but I encourage you to share what happened when you "let go and let God."

Pause for response

Let's take a few moments to reflect and pray.

Lord God, You see all of life; we see minute-sized portions.
    You possess the power of armies; we wait for your hand.
    You give life. We simply live it.

So Father, we thank you. We see your hand. We know your power. Help us sometimes to just let go; to get out of the way and watch you work. Thank you for watching over us here today. We love you. Amen.

Band
Light band; project

Response Song

He Is Lord (chorus, 2nd stanza)

Host
Project announcements

Announcements/Offering

Band with female lead
Light band/project

Featured Music

Abba Father
(by Rebecca St. James)

One adult male, dressed in everyday clothing
Light drama area; project graphic "Just Say the Word" at end

Monologue/Storytelling

"Just Say the Word"

We like to make things pretty complicated. Perhaps freedom can be as simple as knowing that there is a God and I'm not it.

(Change position) There was once a Roman captain who possessed a wonderful staff of highly devoted employees. All wonderful that is, except one prized servant who was suddenly taken very ill, much to the captain's concern. Desperate to save the man's life and remembering recent reports of healing, the captain called for Jesus to come and make his servant well.

Jesus agreed to go. Sickness was pretty much everyday stuff for him; when you're a healer you do what it takes. Go and make house calls. Go and pray. Go and command the dead back to life. But this time it would be different. Simpler.

Jesus made his way toward the sprawling captain's quarters and was stopped by friends of the captain running toward him. Their message was unusual, a word straight from the captain:

"Jesus: Changed my mind. Don't come up after all. I know you're busy; no need for me to take up your time. I'm sure that if you just give the order from right where you are that my servant will come around. I deal with this kind of thing—giving orders, taking orders—a lot. You just say the word."

Jesus was totally blown away. Just say the word? Most people demanded the bedside assistance along with the post-operative care. Just say the word?

It was the first time anyone had seemed to really understand the authority that Jesus possessed; someone who knew what it meant to give orders and take orders, what it meant to know who was really on top.

The messengers found the servant alive and well upon their return; a simple miracle. Jesus never made it to the house. He never met the captain. He never even touched the sick servant. Right there on the road he simply responded to a man who knew that there was a God and he wasn't it. And a word was all it took.

That's simple enough (*looking up to God*); just say the word.

Message

Speaker
Light sermon area

"Blessed Are the Harnessed"

Closing Words

Host
Project worship graphic

Why settle for looking out when you could be looking up. Freedom is about authority. Catch the wind of the Spirit as you run in God's harness this week. Amen.

Exit Music

Band
Light band; maintain graphic

Awesome God

Celebration Thirty

Stamped for the Dance

Felt Need   To discover the lifestyle we're created for

Desired Outcome   To be purposeful in living out balanced godly
                            lifestyles

Theme   Stamped for the Dance (Fall Stewardship Cam-
                            paign)

Word   1 Thessalonians 4:1-7

Metaphor/Image   Our own spirited dance logo: a simple, nongender
                            specific, line drawing of a dancer

Synopsis   We have been created to dance with God. Through
                            all the disciplines of our journey with Christ, we
                            learn the steps of the "Spirited Dance." The next
                            three weekends are our own celebrations of the dis-
                            ciplines, learning the dance steps. In this first cele-
                            bration we set up this overriding dance metaphor
                            and then stamped everyone for the dance at the
                            door.

Enhancement Ideas   This metaphor provides a diversion from the norm
                            and gets one thinking about his/her own dance
                            experiences (teenage apprehension and self-con-
                            sciousness). The opening video clip and the "Satur-
                            day Night Live" cheerleaders sketch hook the
                            audience and identify that "the dance" is a place we
                            all want to go. These celebrations are a homegrown
                            series but certainly represent a theme that could be
                            transferred to other church stewardship events.

Worship Celebration

Opening Music

Band   Instrumental

Light band only; project worship graphic five minutes before each celebration time and continue throughout

Video Clip

Scene of teens entering the dance floor   From "Sixteen Candles"

House lights down; begin immediately following opening music

Call To Worship

Host

Project worship graphic when appropriate

The dance. We all tried to fit in and enjoy ourselves but most of the time we just couldn't. Too shy. Too clumsy. Or maybe just too darned cool.

Today we hear the invitation to another dance. Hear these words from the New Testament:

> "Keep on doing what we told you to do to please God, not in a dogged religious plod, but in a living, spirited dance" (1 Thessalonians 4, *The Message*).

This is the dance you were made for! This is your original identity! God has designed you for this dance. God's made you for this movement. You've been stamped with the imprint of God.

We come to hear from the Lord of the dance, to get in step with the One who designed us to hear his beat and get into the groove. Let's stand now.

Song Celebration

Band

Light band and choir; project words

Day By Day
(by dc talk)

Choir with female lead

Continue lighting; project; no words

Excited About Jesus
(by Brooklyn Tabernacle Choir)

Band

Project words; choir exits following "Day By Day"

Oh, Come Let Us Adore
Day By Day (reprise)

Testimony (unscripted) and Prayer

Host with soft music under

Project speaker or graphic

"Learning To Dance"

Prayer

Let's bow our heads now as we begin a time of prayer.

You may be like I was. You may desperately want to glide gracefully through life, but you don't know the Lord of the dance, the One who made you. Don't pass up the opportunity to seek him this morning. Take time now to tell him that you would like to accept his invitation of love.

Pause for silent response

Maybe you're familiar with the dance, but in the course of even just a week you find yourself getting way out of step. How has it been for you this week? Take a moment to talk to the Lord about where you are and what you would like to change.

Pause for silent response

Lord God, we want to thank you for the moments you give us. We thank you for times when we can be honest and open with you. Thank you that we don't go at this alone. You don't leave us to figure it all out by ourselves. You've come to stay, to live and move and dance in our very lives. We praise you God. Amen.

Stamped for the Dance

Song of Response

Band

Light band and vocalists; project words

It Is Good to Praise the Lord

Announcements/Offering

Host

Featured Music

Three vocalists, two guitars

All are on stools, an "unplugged" feeling
Light center stage; project words for chorus only; graphic otherwise

Lord of the Dance
(UMH, # 261)

Drama

One male, one female   "The Cheerleaders"
House lights down; light center stage; project players

Two cheerleaders are sitting on bench looking excited, wiping their brows.

Arianna   Craig! Our dream come true. Here we are cheering for the big dance. I can hardly contain myself. But, Craig . . . Oh my gosh, Craig. You have a, a, tie on. It's very nice, but, well, a little different. Did you wear it to try to fit in at the dance?

Craig   No, Arianna. I did not wear it for that reason, Arianna. I wore it because we have a great speaker today *(insert name of speaker, who is wearing a tie)* and I just thought I should show some support.

Arianna: Oh! that's very nice Craig. Craig, it's time! *(They get in place for the cheer.)*

Both   Well we are cheering,
                Cause it's our dream
                It's good for raising
                Our self-esteem!

Arianna   I'm Arianna,
                and I am movin'
                Here at the dance,
                my feet are groovin'!

Craig   My name is Craig,
                and I am *rumblin, (substitute word that rhymes with speaker's name)*
                I'm ready to shout,
                for my friend *the pastor (substitute name of speaker)*

Both   Okey Dokey!!!!!!! *(They sit back down and mop heads.)*

Craig   Arianna—I hate to be the one to tell you this, but you have lipstick on your teeth. *(Arianna is upset.)*

Craig   I'm sorry, Arianna! *(Together they try to get the lipstick off.)*

Arianna	It's OK; It just . . . hurts.
Craig	But Arianna, I only share that kind of stuff with my closest friends.
Arianna	Really?
Craig	Yeah! *(They hug.)*
Arianna	Craig, did you get stamped?
Craig	Stamped?
Arianna	Yea. Stamped for the dance.
Craig	Oh! Stamped for the dance! Sure I did. It's right here. *(He pulls up his sleeve to reveal his bicep.)*
Arianna	Gee; I never thought of having it put on my arm.
Craig	Yeah, I've always wanted a tattoo but my Dad . . .
Arianna	Your dad . . . *(pointing)*
Craig	Yeah, my dad . . .
Arianna	Wants you. Your dad wants you.
Craig	Oh. *(Turns to stand and look out to his dad.)* Yes, Father? No I did not get a tattoo. Yes, I will be home by 10:30. A picture? Sure. *(They pose together.)*
Arianna	Craig—oh my gosh, Craig! I know what they need to get this spirited dance going!
Craig	Arianna! Are you thinking what I'm thinking?
Both	The perfect cheer! Let's rock the house!

Music begins for cheer (perhaps "Staying Alive" by the BeeGees)

They exit after about sixty seconds and music fades

Fade lights when players leave stage

Speaker
Light sermon area

Message

"Stamped for the Dance"

Pastor-led
Light altar; project worship graphic; band plays instrumental

Communion

Host

Closing Words

Don't settle for sitting on the sidelines. This is the dance you were created for. Get in step with God and allow God to show you all that life was meant to be. Amen

Project worship graphic

Band
Light band; maintain graphic

Exit Music

Day By Day

Get On Your Feet

Felt Need	To feel like a part of what God is doing
Desired Outcome	To hear God's call to us for mission, ministry, and service
Theme	Spirited Dance: Get on Your Feet
Word	Psalm 123:1-2
Metaphor/Image	Drums of all kinds
Synopsis	This second weekend in our "Spirited Dance" series focuses first on hearing the beat that is worship, and then getting up and acting on what we hear—serving in mission. Christianity is not a spectator sport! A number of great pieces make this a wonderful celebration, and the live high school drum corp marching in from the back of the sanctuary was a definite "wow" factor.
Enhancement Ideas	We placed drum sets on the platform, and drums were on the altar. As exciting as the music and live drumline are, the highest point comes as we connect with the message—that we can listen to the beat of God's drum, get up, and make it happen! No spectators here!

Worship Celebration

Opening Beat

Drum Line
Project worship graphic; band in place with precelebration lighting; drum line from area high school begins playing in foyer and marches in, up center aisle and divides in front to ascend onto extension from both sides; they play a bit and then exit through curtained doorways; house band picks up beat before they leave and segues into "Get On Your Feet"; worship team initiates standing and clapping concurrently

Opening Music

Band with female lead
Light band; maintain graphic; no words projected

Get On Your Feet
(by Gloria Estefan)

Call To Worship

Host
Maintain graphic

Worship is anything but a spectator sport. Out of the chaos of our lives we come to listen, to actually feel the beat of God, the one who challenges us to get up, get on our feet and serve. We come to offer ourselves for loving action in the rhythm of the dance—the Spirited Dance.

Today is about service; hearing the beat of God and letting that beat drive us out to serve in Jesus' name. Let's continue to worship now as we sing.

Song Celebration

Band
Light band; project words

Come Into This House (Carmen)
Almighty

Prayer

Host talks and three persons, read scripture from the floor (project responses marked in bold below); Soft music under

This morning we continue to celebrate the Spirited Dance. As we come to a time of prayer we want to concentrate on hearing the rhythm together, to listen and reflect on what it means to be servants who gain energy by listening for the beat of the drummer, the Lord of the Dance. We need to look up and hear the beat to be able to go out and serve. Let that be our unified prayer this morning. Will you say these words with me?

Lord I want to be your servant. I need to hear the beat. *(Leader may need to repeat this phrase.)*

Now hear these words of Jesus as we continue to reflect together.

Reader 1   "This is a large work I've called you into, but don't be overwhelmed by it. It's best to start small. Give a cool cup of water to someone who is thirsty, for instance. The smallest act of giving or receiving makes you a true apprentice. You won't lose out on a thing" (from Matthew 10, *The Message*).

Lord I want to be your servant. I need to hear the beat.

Reader 2   So Jesus got them together to settle things down. He said, "You've observed how godless rulers throw their weight around, how quickly a little power goes to their heads. It's not going to be that way with you. Whoever wants to be great must become a servant. Whoever wants to be first among you must be your slave. That is what the Son of Man has done: He came to serve, not be served— and then to give away his life in exchange for the many who are held hostage" (from Matthew 20, *The Message).*

Lord I want to be your servant. I need to hear the beat.

Reader 3   "Then [they] are going to say, 'Master, what are you talking about? When did we ever see you hungry and feed you, thirsty and give you a drink? And when did we ever see you sick or in prison and come to you?' Then the King will say, 'I'm telling the solemn truth: Whenever you did one of these things to someone overlooked or ignored, that was me—you did it to me'" (from Matthew 25, *The Message*).

Lord I want to be your servant. I need to hear the beat.

(Host)   Lord, we live in a world of noise, a world of voices calling for our attention. We need to hear you Jesus. We need to hear and recognize the sound of your beat calling us to service. The beat calls us, not just to occasional good acts but to servant lifestyles; lives laid down in anticipation of what you will do through us. Help us Lord. Forgive our numbing preoccupation with ourselves—our tendency toward navel-gazing—and make us into offerings sold out to your agenda. Hear now this prayer of our hearts as we sing.

Song of Response

Host
Light band; project words

We Are an Offering

Announcements/Offering

Host

Featured Music

Band with male lead
Light band; project with worship graphic intermittentlty

Lord of the Dance
(by Steven Curtis Chapman)

Get On Your Feet

Message

Speaker   "Get On Your Feet"
*Light sermon area; drum line begins playing in back hall on cue and comes into sanctuary when speaker is finishing;
after a brief drill the band again segues into "Get On Your Feet"; drum line finishes and exits*

Exit Music

Band   Get On Your Feet
Light band; project worship graphic

God's Toolbox/Miracles Happen: An Advent Celebration

Felt Need	To live "bigger" lives
Desired Outcome	To believe that God works in ordinary people, including us
Theme	Everyday People/God's Toolbox
Word	Luke 1:30-34
Metaphor/Image	Toolbox with ordinary miracle tools—water, dirt, bread, etc.
Synopsis	This is a favorite celebration for a number of reasons, but mostly because of the message that God makes miracles using ordinary objects in regular places with everyday people. God's Toolbox provides a great metaphor to rethink the simple tools God really uses to accomplish the miraculous. This is a great message of hope for our "mundane" lives.
Enhancement Ideas	On the altar table consider placing a long, old-fashioned wooden toolbox with some water in a jar, dirt in a crock, basic tools, broken bread, and candles all tucked inside. (The toolbox caught on fire during the Call To Worship once, proving that worship is a risky business!) Two music pieces, "Everyday People" and "Waiting for Lightning" are extremely powerful. Weave the monologue from a young, modern Mary into the "Waiting" piece. A wonderful Advent celebration!

Worship Celebration

Opening Music

Band

House lights low; light band

Everyday People
(by Sly and the Family Stone)

Call To Worship/Candle lighting

Host

House lights up; project worship graphic; Host asks congregation to stand

"God's Tool Box"

What does it take to make a miracle happen? Our own limited perspectives fancy God with sparkling magic potions carefully arranged in a glittering heavenly toolbox. Maybe a few wands thrown in for the tough jobs.

But God's best work has been done using amazingly ordinary stuff. Water, mud, spit, a piece of stale bread, a barn, a teenage girl. Ordinary objects in regular places, with everyday people. Miracles happen when the divine intersects with the ordinary.

Host lights the first Advent candle

We come to explore the possibility that any one of us could be expecting a miracle, so don't count yourself out. Stand with me now in worship as we open ourselves to what God wants to do.

Song Celebration

Band

Light band; project words

O Come All Ye Faithful
(UMH, # 234)
I Waited for the Lord On High

Prayer

Host
Return to worship graphic; soft music under final portion

We so often look up to see God, expecting to find God in the sky. We forget that the Divine comes in the ordinary. We neglect to look around. We fail to see God in each other.

Miracles are waiting to happen with ordinary objects, in regular places, through everyday people. We need to learn to look for and pray for the miraculous to occur here in one another.

Before we pray together, let's take time to greet one another and affirm the God who has come to be present in all our lives. Greet those around you now.

Pause for greeting time

You may be seated. And now let's pray together for one another.

Jesus, thank you for coming to this ordinary place. Thank you for living in us as everyday people. Sometimes we've failed to see you because we've neglected to look. Lord God, we pray, not just for our own selves, but for those we touched and spoke to today. As this season of Christmas begins, let no one go away without knowing that you want to do divine work in them, that you want to birth a miracle as awesome and as ordinary as the birth of Jesus. Lord, let none of us here today be satisfied until the miracle in our lives is carried full-term and birthed. We trust you, Lord, to make our lives all they were meant to be. Thank you for choosing to work with the ordinary. Amen.

Song Of Response

There Is a Redeemer

Band
Light band; project words

Announcements/Offering

Host

Featured Music and Drama

Band with male lead

House lights down; at end of second chorus lights up on drama area for monologue (guitar continues); project player

Waiting for Lightning
(by Steven Curtis Chapman)

Monologue

Female teen

"Waiting for Lightning"

A teenage, modern-day Mary is seated on stage in a chair in her bedroom. A wedding gown hangs on a hook. She is intermittently journaling and thinking out loud, alternating between standing and sitting.

(writing) I can't believe everything that's happened today. Believe, comprehend, whatever. I've got to get a hold of this and deal with it, to make some sense out of it all.

I'm sure it wasn't a dream. I'm sure I heard the voice, *(looks up as though remembering)* "Mary, you're going to have a son. He'll be God's son; the Messiah."

(back to the journal) And that's when it begins not to make sense anymore . . . *(out to the audience)* I mean, I'm the queen of ordinary. This town I call home is way past nowhere. *(getting up on her feet)* I never even thought the Messiah would come in my lifetime, let alone through these ninety-eight pounds.

(looking up) Oh God, one minute I trust and the next minute I doubt.

Part of me is the little girl who has always loved you,

And part of me is the woman, too scared to let love give birth.

For a moment I feel the excitement of a world that will at last know it's Savior—and then I shrink back. They'll stare. I'll get so huge. I'll feel so ashamed.

You know me God. I've always prayed for the miracle, longed for the Messiah. But I thought it would look different. I thought *He* would look different. I've waited for lightning—some cosmic clap of thunder to prove yourself to me . . . but you were quietly whispering my name. *(sits back down to begin journaling while song is finished)*

Message

"Miracles Happen"

Speaker
Light sermon area

Monologue Conclusion

Same player (Mary)
House lights down; lights up on player on cue after sermon (sermon lights down); project player

I see it all now God; I was yours before, and nothing's really changed. Whatever you want . . . I'm ready.

Closing Words

Host
Bring house lights up slowly; project worship graphic

Don't be caught waiting for lightning. Go now, and expect that God will use the ordinary to create the miraculous through everyday people. Amen.

Exit Music

Waiting for Lightning

Band
Light band; project worship graphic

The Cosmic Party: Everybody In: An Advent Celebration

Felt Need	To belong and be loved
Desired Outcome	To understand that God's desire for ALL to know Him
Theme	The Cosmic Party: Everybody In
Word	Luke 14:16-17
Metaphor/Image	Helium balloons and party decor
Synopsis	Long before Wayne and Garth from "Wayne's World" ever spoke the words "party on," Jesus himself brought this greeting to the world. It is the message of Christmas announcing that a great cosmic party is going on and everyone is invited. Christians, however, err on the side of making exclusive guest lists and wind up inviting only those who resemble themselves. This celebration speaks the radical Christmas message that everyone deserves an invitation to the party.
Enhancement Ideas	Consider inflating huge bunches of gold, red, and green helium balloons to float all over the sanctuary creating a definite party atmosphere. A highlight of this celebration is the piece that emerges as a combination of testimony, pictures of a recent youth group trip to New York City, and the moving song "See Me, Feel Me." Using the testimony and pictures interwoven with the song communicates this message of compassion for those who have yet to receive an invitation to the party.

Worship Celebration

Opening Music

Band/female lead
Light band and extension; project worship graphic

Joy to the World
(by Mariah Carey)

Call To Worship/Candle lighting

Host
Project worship graphic; band assembles on stools

"The Invitation"

If you were throwing a party, one of the first things you'd do would be to make a guest list. The list would be about whom to include—but of course, that means it would also be about whom *not* to include. Today we're invited to a great cosmic party: God's party. Unlike us, God has always refused to make a guest list. Everything in God resists turning anyone away from the party.

On this third week of Advent, we participate in God's open invitation to all who would come and celebrate the birth that so clearly stated God's intention:

Not joy to those who have it all together
Not joy to those we know and feel comfortable around
But joy . . . to the world!

And now in the spirit of Christ the King, let's sing the simple songs of Christmas. Relax and remain seated as we enjoy this time.

Carol Celebration

Band
Light band; project words; lower house lights

Silent Night
(UMH, #239)
What Child Is This
(UMH, #219)
O Little Town of Bethlehem
(UMH, #230)

Prayer

Host
Continue lighting; project worship graphic; soft music under (guitar)

Lord, we sing and are reminded that you went totally out of your way to include us. You refused to rest easy until you could come into our world and become one of us. And now you continue to stretch out your hand, to open your heart of love to include as many as will come.

Lord, as your servants we want to be available to you as part of your invitation to others. Change our inward focus. Forgive us. We've been takers, not givers. We've made guest lists when you distinctly said "everybody in." Give us your heart of love to care for others. Teach us to see others as you do through eyes of concern and acceptance, just as you did by sending Jesus. Thank you! Amen.

Announcements/Offering

Host

Special Feature

Band with one vocal lead
One teen speaks intermittently her own
edited description of a recent trip to New York
to serve in soup kitchens
Light drama area and band; house lights down

Project New York pictures as appropriate or replace with your own experience

"See Me, Feel Me"
(by The Who, from "Tommy")

Speaker
Light sermon area

Message

"The Cosmic Party: Everybody In"

Band
Light band; project worship graphic

Exit Music

Joy to the World

Celebration Thirty-four

The Christmas Promise: An Advent Celebration

Felt Need	To know the God who keeps promises
Desired Outcome	To begin acting on the promises God has made
Theme	The Christmas Promise
Word	Luke 1:41-42, 45
Metaphor/Image	Cradle with lighted candle positioned inside
Synopsis	While Christmas is often a season that reminds people of broken promises and unfulfilled dreams, the good news is that our God is the Great Promise Keeper. Jesus represents God's best fulfilling promise of a Savior to us. We also use this wonderful celebration as an opportunity to experience baptism and dedication of infants, our act of faith that God will continue to fulfill the promise of life to us and our children.
Enhancement Ideas	Use a candle positioned inside a baby's cradle as a way of visualizing the Christmas promise in the form of a display on the platform. Lots of simple candles adorning the altar table are powerful. The music is excellent and meaningful throughout, creating a truly memorable Christmas service.
Featured Option	Infant baptism and/or dedication

Advent Worship Celebration

Opening Music

Band with female lead
Light band; Christmas graphics; lower house lights

Happy Christmas

Call To Worship

Host
Project worship graphic

Christmas presents a lot of challenges for us—finding perfect gifts, creating perfect celebrations, and spending time with not-so-perfect people. Yet those challenges may not be nearly as difficult as our need to find a place of hope when nothing is quite how we had pictured it should be. Christmas can be an annual reminder of broken family relationships, unfulfilled personal dreams, unanswered prayers that can leave us with but two choices: to believe in only what we see around us, or to put our total trust in the God who *always* keeps promises. To find and renew our faith for what God alone will do.

And so on this fourth Sunday of Advent we come to find new hope in the One who not only kept the great promise of a Savior, but continues to keep all the promises made to God's own. Stand with me now as we celebrate together.

Carol Celebration

Band and Choir
Choir enters at beginning; light band and choir; project words

Arise, Shine
The First Noel

Baptisms/Dedications

Host introduces
Light altar; soft music under introduction; "Jesus, Born On This Day; project close-ups of infants entire time

Something we do here each year at Christmas time is allow the opportunity for parents and the congregation to offer their children to the Lord, understanding that these children truly belong to God and trusting that God's promise will be fulfilled as we do all in our ability to raise them in Christ-centered homes. As we enter into this celebration, we pray for these children and rejoice with their families in the ongoing mark of God on their lives.

(To the parents) As a witness to the body of Christ, let me ask you to state your commitment. Do you believe in the Bible as contained in the Old and New Testaments? Have you accepted Jesus as your personal Savior? Will you raise your child in a home that centers around Christ so that, when they are old enough, they may be better prepared to accept Christ for themselves? If so, answer "we do."

(To the congregation) Will you be an example to these children, as their surrogate spiritual parents, so that they will see Christ in you? If so, answer "we do."

Begin song: "Jesus, Born On This Day"

Prayer

Host

Will you bow with me as we pray together?

We all find certain situations in our lives when it's really tough to believe in God. Possibly there is an area in your life that you cannot imagine even God being able to work out. What in your life seems hopeless? Perhaps you just can't see your now-grown baby boy or girl ever knowing Jesus personally. Maybe you are emotionally drained or filled with the harrowing image of numerous unfulfilled dreams. You might be overwhelmed by bills, agendas, or hurting relationships and can hardly perceive God caring enough to be concerned about your feelings or predicament.

But we serve a God of hope who always keeps promises. *(small pause)* Right now as we focus on God's desire to be our everything, silently name your concern and leave it in God's hands.

Pause for silent prayer

Father God, into the empty places in our lives, devastated by broken promises and vacated by faithless companions, come Lord Jesus, as companion and comforter. We cry out to you for healing and hope. We desire to act in confidence, knowing that you fulfill all your promises. We look to you as the ultimate Promise, the true fulfillment of all our Christmas dreams. Amen.

Concurrent Music

Choir and Kids

Light band and choirs; project worship graphic and kids intermittently

Jesus, Born On This Day
(by Mariah Carey)

Song Of Response

Band

A capella; light band and choir; project words

Yet In Thy Dark Streets
(2nd stanza, "O Little Town,"
UMH, #230)

Video

Christmas TV Promotion
House lights down; begin immediately

Featured Music

Choir and Band

Light band and choir immediately; choir exits following

O Holy Night

Speaker
Sermon light set; with graphics and one video clip

Message

"The Christmas Promise"

Speaker
Project worship graphic

Closing Words

Band
Light band; Christmas graphics

Exit Music

Happy Christmas

Appendix A: Songs and Hymns

Song Title	Artist	Compact Disc	Label	WC#
Abba Father	Rebecca St. James	God	Forefront	29
Ain't No Mountain High Enough	Diana Ross	Ultimate Call	Motown	25
Almighty	Wayne Watson	Home Free	Word Music	11, 31
Almighty God	Tom Ketke	Calvary's Love	Word Music	23
Always	Paul Baloche	He Is Faithful	Integrity's Hosanna! Music	18
Arise, Shine	Steven Upspringer		Priesthood Publications	34
Awesome God	Rich Mullins	Awesome God	Edwards Grand Corp, Inc.	29
Ball and Chain	Susan Ashton	Wakened by the Wind	Birdwing Music	13
Because You Loved Me	Celine Dion	Titanic	Realsongs	16, 17
Blessed Be the Name of the Lord	Integrity Music	Perfect Peace	Integrity/Word Music	5, 15, 29
Breathe In Me	Michael W. Smith	I'll Lead You Home	O'Ryan Music	7
Butterfly Kisses	Bob Carlisle	Shades of Grace	Diadem	18, 20
Carry Me High	Rebecca St. James	God	Forefront	23
Celebration	Kool and the Gang	Celebrate	Poly Gram Records	3, 12, 28
Change the World	Eric Clapton	Phenomenon	Reprise Records	22
Choose Your Tomorrow	Tamara Batarseh	Love in the Real World		11
Come Into This House	Carmen	Addicted to Jesus	Chordant Dist.	2, 31
Come Just as You Are	Maranatha	Praise Classics: Lord of Lords	Wor Ent	26
Create In Me a Clean Heart	Integrity Music	Perfect Peace	Integrity's Hosanna! Music	25
Day By Day	Various	Godspell	Arista Records	7, 30
Don't Look Away	Gary Adrian	Simple Faith	Independent Label	8
Everybody Hurts	R.E.M.	Automatic for the People	R.E.M./Athens, Ltd.	2
Everyday People	Sly and the Family Stone	Stand	Epic Record	32

Song	Artist	Album	Label	Page
Excited About Jesus	Brooklyn Tabernacle Choir	Live: We Come Rejoicing	Diadem Music BMI	23, 30
Fire of God	Vineyard	Refiner's Fire	Chordant Dist.	21
Get On Your Feet	Gloria Estefan	Cuts Both Ways	CBS Records, Inc.	31
Glorify thy Name	Various	Prayers and Worship	Chordant Dist.	21
Great Is the Lord	Michael W. Smith	The Wonder Years	Meadowgreen Music	3
Happy Christmas	Rebecca St. James	Christmas	Forefront	34
He Is Lord	Ca Tornquist	Angel Praise	Chordant Dist. Group	29
Heart of Gold	Neil Young	Harvest	Reprise Records	25
Heaven Is In My Heart	Graham Kendrick	Highest Place	Integrity's Hosanna! Music	18, 26
Holy Ground	Geron Davis	Send It on Up	Meadowgreen Music	17
Holy Is the Lord	Tom Fetke	Exalt Him	Word Entertainment	12
Holy, Holy, Holy		*UM Hymnal #64*		17, 29
Honesty	Billy Joel	52nd Street	Columbia Records	26
Hope Set High	Amy Grant	Heart in Motion	Age to Age Music, Inc.	3
How Priceless	Vineyard Music	Words of Worship	Chordant Dist. Group	1
I Am Not Ashamed	Brooklyn Tabernacle Choir	Live: We Come Rejoicing	Diadem Music BMI	7
I Believe in You	Bob Dylan	Slow Train Coming	Columbia Records	11
I Got the One I Want	Amy Grant	Songs From the Loft	Age to Age Music, Inc.	13
I Love You Lord	Laurie Klein	Exalt Him V.2	House of Mercy Marantha! Music	9, 27, 29
I Waited for the Lord on High	Bill Batstone	A Little Broken Bread	Marathon Music	5, 7, 26, 32
I Want to Be Where You Are	Hosanna Music	Hosanna Music Sampler	Word Ernt	28
I Want to Know You	Vineyard Music	Hear Our City	Chardant Dist. Group	3
I Will Call on the Lord	Michael O'Shields		Sounds III, Inc.	13
I Worship You	Jim Cowan	I Worship You	East West Records	9
I'll Be There for You	The Rembrandts	F.R.I.E.N.D.S	East	20
I'll Lead You Home	Michael W. Smith	I'll Lead You Home	O'Ryan Music	7
I'm Coming Out	Diana Ross	All the Greatest Hits	Motown	23
If It Makes You Happy	Sheryl Crow	Tuesday Night Music Club	A&M Records	4
In the Light	DC Talk	Jesus Freak	Forefront	23

Song Title	Artist	Compact Disc	Label	WC#
In This House	Christ Church Choir	Hand in Hand	Century Oak Publishing	4
It Is Good to Praise the Lord	Maranatha Music	Long Play Thanksgiving	Word Ent.	30
Jesus Is Just All Right With Me	The Doobie Brothers	Best of the Doobies	Warner Bros., Inc.	21, 27
Jesus, Born on This Day	Mariah Carey	Christmas Album	Columbia	34
Joy to the World	Mariah Carey	Christmas Album	Columbia	33
Joyful, Joyful We Adore Thee		UM Hymnal #89		14
Let Your Healing Love	Vineyard Music	Worship Song of Vineyard	Chordant Dist. Group	4
Like a Child	Jars of Clay	Jars of Clay	Pogostick Music	5
Lord I Lift Your Name on High	Rick Founds	Hymns and Choruses v. 4	Maranatha! Music	12, 21, 26
Lord of the Dance	Steven Curtis Chapman	Signs of Life	Chordant Dist. Music	30, 31
Lord You Are More Precious	Y. Anderson	Songs	Songs and Creations Pub.	25
Love Has a Hold on Me	Amy Grant	House of Love	Age to Age Music, Inc.	28
Love Is What We've Come Here For	Michael W. Smith	Songs From the Loft	Reunion Rec.	20
My Life Is in Your Hands	Kathy Trocoli	Kathy Trocoli	Provident Music	1
My Place in This World	Michael W. Smith	Go West Young Man	Provident Music	2
No Other Name	Robert Gay	Victors Crown	Hosanna! Music	21
O Come All Ye Faithful		UM Hymnal #234		32
O Holy Night	Integrity Music	Praise Magnific	Integrity/Word	34
O Little Town of Bethlehem		UM Hymnal #230		33
Oh Lord, You're Beautiful	Keith Green	So You Want to Go Back to Egypt	Birdwing Music	26
Oh, Come Let Us Adore Him	Hosanna Music	Praise Worship v. 3	Integrity/Word Ent.	30
One Less Stone	Brooklyn Tabernacle Choir	Live: We Come Rejoicing	Diadem Music BMI	17, 23
One Voice	Maranatha Music	Together for the Gospel	Maranatha! Music	16
Only Here a Little While	Billy Dean	Greatest Hits	Liberty 6	22
Only Your Love	Margaret Becker	Grace	Group/Richwood Music/BMI	1, 4, 16
Open Our Eyes	Bob Cull		Maranatha! Music	7
Rejoice	Sec. Chap. Acts	Rejoice	Chordant Dist. Group	18, 22

Title	Artist	Album	Publisher	No.
Road to Zion	Petra	More Power to Ya	Word Ent.	6
Say the Name	Margaret Becker	Soul	Chordant Dist., Music	21
Seek First	Amy Grant	Songs From the Loft	Age to Age Music, Inc.	8, 11
Shine On Us	Phillips, Craig and Dean	My Utmost for His Highest	Word Ent.	15, 22
Show Me the Way	Styx	Edge of the Century	A & M Records	14
Signs	Tesla	5 Man Accoustical Jam	Gesser Records	12
Silent Night		UM Hymnal #239		33
Sing a Joyful Song	Acoustic Worship	Love of God	Maranatha! Music	28
Somewhere Over the Rainbow	Dino	Kartsonakis	Provident	20
Stand and See	Praise Band	Praise Band 5	Word Ent.	25
Standing Outside the Fire	Garth Brooks	In Pieces	Criterion Music Corp.	9
Still Haven't Found What I'm Looking For	U2	Joshua Tree	Chappel	5
Surely the Presence	Various	Prayers and Worship	Chordant Dist.	17, 20
Sweet, Sweet Spirit	Homecoming/Gathering	This Is My Spirit	Chordant Dist.	17
Take Up Your Cross	Brooklyn Tabernacle Choir	Live: We Come Rejoicing	Diadem Music BMI	6
Teach Your Children Well	Crosby, Stills, and Nash	So Far	Atlantic Records	18
That's Just the Way It Is	Bruce Hornsby and the Range	The Way It Is	RCA Records	12
The Feast	Hosanna Music	Amazing Love	Integrity/Word	1
The First Noel	Buchanan	Noel	Adoration Inc.	34
The Gift				1
The Power	Amy Grant	House of Love	Reunion Rec.	15
The Power of Love	Huey Lewis and the News	Heart of Rock and Roll	Chrysalis Records	16
There Is a Redeemer	Keith Green	Songs for the Shepherd	Chordant Dist.	32
There's Freedom in You	Gary Adrian	Simple Faith	Independent Label	8
Treasure	Gary Chapman	The Light Inside	Word Music Group	14
Trust and Obey		UM Hymnal #467		11
Turn Your Eyes Upon Jesus		UM Hymnal #349		22

Song Title	Artist	Compact Disc	Label	WC#
Waiting for Lightning	Steven Curtis Chapman	Live Adventure	Star Song	32
We Are an Offering	Dwight Liles		Word Music, Inc.	31
We Believe in God	Amy Grant	Songs From the Loft	Age to Age Music, Inc.	13, 21, 27
We Come to Praise You	Amy Grant	Songs From the Loft	Age to Age Music, Inc.	20, 28
We Declare Your Majesty	Malcolm DuPlessis		Maranatha Praise, Inc.	14
We Exalt You	Hosanna	See His Glory	Integrity/Word	14
We Need Jesus	Petra	Petra Praise 2	Word Music Group	12, 16
What a Friend	Lee Behnken	Jesus Is God	Bob-A-Lee Productions	6
What Child Is This		*UM Hymnal* #219		33
Where Do I Go?	Amy Grant	Songs From the Loft	Age to Age Music, Inc.	8, 11, 27
Worship You	Rick Riso		Word Music, Inc.	19, 28
You Were There	Brooklyn Tabernacle Choir	Live: We Come Rejoicing	Diadem Music BMI	27

Appendix B: Web Sites for Resources

Integrity Music — need to order software from *www.integritymusic.com*

Christian Copyright License (CCLI) — Go to their website @ *www.ccli.com*. Click on appropriate location (i.e. North America). Click on License holder services, then enter CCLI# and Zip code then click on Song Select Online. This will give you information on the songs and you can also obtain some song lyrics from this Web site.

Worship Leader — Their website is: *www.worshipleaders.org*. Click on their index or search icon.

Hosanna! Music — You will need to order software from their Web site: *www.hosannamusic.com*. Go to ministry links icon then Worship Resource. Worship software can be ordered from there.

Maranatha! Music — Their Web site is *www.maranathamusic.com*. Click on audio catalog icon then the appropriate icon from there (i.e. New Releases, Praise Classics, etc.).

CD-ROM Installation Instructions

For detailed installation instructions on viewing the interactive demo and the catalog of images included on the CD-ROM, please see pages 11-12.